MW00658551

MENTORING *in the* ENSEMBLE ARTS

Helping Others Find Their Voice

MENTORING *in the* ENSEMBLE ARTS

Helping Others Find Their Voice

With Appreciation

TIM SHARP

Tim Sharp

GIA Publications, Inc.
Chicago

Mentoring in the Ensemble Arts:
Helping Others Find Their Voice
Tim Sharp

G-7961

ISBN: 978-1-57999-835-6
Copyright © 2011 GIA Publications, Inc.
7404 S. Mason Avenue, Chicago, Illinois 60638
www.giamusic.com
All rights reserved. Printed in the United States of America.

To

William Darby Sharp

and

Janette Sharp

CONTENTS

Maturity begins to grow when you can sense your concern for others outweighing your concern for yourself.

—John MacNaughton

RECITATIVE

The Mentoring Environment of the Ensemble

True heroism is remarkably sober, very undramatic. It is not the urge to surpass all at whatever cost, but the urge to serve others at whatever cost.

—Arthur Ashe

The experience of mentor and protégé is much the same as the experience of parent and child. At every moment, I am simultaneously the child of my mother and father and the parent of my child. I am forever in debt for the lessons I learned from my parents, and will forever be willing to guide and remain available to offer helpful lessons to my daughter. Both roles teach me something of the giving process—one role in how to give, the other role in how to receive.

Similarly, the experience of mentor and protégé is much the same as the experience of teacher and student-learner. At every moment, I am both a learner of new material and lessons and a teacher of knowledge gained and lessons learned. I am forever in debt for the lessons I learned from my teachers, and I remain eager to bring continuity to my profession by passing those lessons on to my students and sharing ways to apply those lessons, which I developed in my own experience. Both roles work to make me a better student-learner and a better teacher.

However, the experience of mentor and protégé is different from the experience of parent–child and teacher–student-learner. The mentor–protégé experience has much in common with the latter two roles, but there are important differences. The mentor and protégé are generally not connected or motivated by a genetic connection, and as pure and noble as it may be, the mentor and protégé are generally not connected to each other due to an academic or business contract.

The objective of *Mentoring in the Ensemble Arts* is to acknowledge and learn from the similarities in these various roles, to note the differences, but more significantly, to highlight the uniqueness of the mentor–protégé relationship in the ensemble arts. The mentor–protégé relationship constitutes a separate sphere of influence—learning and trust. The purpose of this book is to apply both the similarities and the differences to the advancement of the mentor–protégé relationship specifically within the context of the musical ensemble.

This book is prompted by a unique moment in the educational experience when walls, barriers, divisions, and categories of learning are being torn down. It is written at a time when organizational staffing charts are becoming flat and at a time when community experiences are becoming rare. Personal learning communities are replacing former forms of continuing education. And while brick and mortar buildings, classrooms, textbooks, school buses, and faculty lounges are still an important part of the extended educational process, at the same time, personal learning communities, wikis, social networks, digital downloads, and significantly, the mentor–protégé relationship, are each a growing part of the new learning and professional development reality.

It is my wish that everyone could feel that they have the greatest job on earth. In such a perfect world, everyone's gifts and source for fulfillment would be perfectly matched to the work they perform and the way they spend their days. In my life, such a match exists between my vocation and my interests and source of professional fulfillment—I observe people as they work with musical ensembles. This is my job.

As Executive Director of the American Choral Directors Association, I literally observe hundreds of conductors and ensembles each year as they rehearse and perform. In this work, I am observing an artistic and social activity that has existed in community for centuries.

Not long ago and in a country outside the United States, I attempted to explain to a young taxi driver taking me from the airport to a conference I was attending, why I was there and what I did for a living. After explaining I was a choral conductor and I was visiting to hear choral performances at a choral conference, he responded to me in English in a thick accent, "You work in an ancient profession." He is right, of course, and he cut right to the core of my profession. In addition, his observation is one of the reasons for writing this book.

As I observe conductors and ensembles, including my own ensembles, I have not only observed wonderful music being made, but also observed lives being built. I hear life lessons taught and personal experiences shared that go much deeper than the coaching of pitches and rhythms within an ensemble setting. And while material sound is very much the immediate reason for being in a music ensemble, human emotion and shared meaning is every bit as important a part of the nuance of the rehearsal and performance setting for both conductor and ensemble member.

The community known to musicians as an ensemble is both a vibrant learning environment and a subtle mentoring environment. The fact that the ensemble is part of, in the words of my taxi driver, an "ancient profession," obscures the fact that in the 21st century the musical ensemble emerges as a robust learning community and social organization. The discipling environment for the mentor–protégé is constantly present within the musical ensemble, under our noses, yet possibly and most likely completely invisible and unacknowledged.

The intent of *Mentoring in the Ensemble Arts* is to acknowledge the unacknowledged setting of the musical ensemble as a very rich environment for the mentor–protégé experience to exist and flourish. The musical ensemble is a profound resource—

available and operational on a regular and recurring basis—for both unintentional as well as intentional mentoring. The process of learning notes, tuning harmonies, and balancing sounds can be applied as a metaphor for life lessons the conductor shares with the ensemble and that ensemble members can share with other ensemble members. Additionally, as a singer in a choir was recently observed writing on her choral folder, "music is my mentor."

Acknowledgments

It can often be intimidating to offer personal acknowledgments at the outset of any creative effort, but particularly for a book about mentoring. Mentors have shaped every positive aspect of my life, my thinking, my education, and my vocation and career. The great fear is that I might omit a person, ensemble, experience, book, or any of the many individuals who have had such an influence.

Acknowledgment, however, represents the reason I am passionate about the topic of mentoring and the reason I hope to raise additional awareness and perpetuate the importance of mentoring within the setting of the musical ensemble.

The focus of *Mentoring in the Ensemble Arts*, and the element that distinguishes this study and reflection from other studies on the topic, is the added environment of the musical ensemble. Throughout my life, the musical setting of the ensemble rehearsal room has been my incubator; so while it could be intimidating to think about *all* of my mentors in life, writing this book has emboldened me by limiting the scope to only those who mentored me within the ensemble arts.

I thank my mentoring father and mother, W. D. (William Darby) and Janette Estep Sharp. Genetically, I have my father's tenor voice, almost literally. To hear him talk is to hear me talk. I can still see and hear him opting for the high ending on the hymns we sang together in church when I was a child, one of the largest ensembles in which I continue to participate as a protégé. My father's passion for people, life, and family as he worked with church congregations will forever inspire me in the living out of my life. I knew early in life that my mother loved the singing voice, and loved to sing. Her voice was refined and she modeled a love for singing for me. She also wanted a piano in the house and as a result I cannot remember a time when a piano was not present in our home. My mother is the reason I took piano lessons and, more significantly, my mother is the reason I never quit piano. The piano of my childhood is in my office today.

I thank my elementary school teachers for recognizing that music and art were important to me as a child and important in early childhood development. It is not a mystery to me that I still remember them now by name as well as by musical experience—Mary Ewin Hadden, Audrey Cox, Gertrude Lucas, Lucille Brooks, Chester Marie Alcott, Bethel Hatfield. They nurtured my love for music in church, school, and community, and incorporated music into many of my learning activities. I still recall important lessons through musical experiences offered by non-specialist teachers in my early school years. I cannot imagine what the confusing process of growing up would have been like without music as a mentor, and I thank my early childhood teachers for knowing that music is a natural part of life and learning.

I thank my junior high school band teacher, Robert Martin, for his endless patience as I struggled to learn to play the clarinet when what I really wanted to play was the saxophone. I thank my high school choral teacher, Jane Dressler, for rescuing me from the course that would have represented my only failing grade in my scholastic history (chemistry) by suggesting I take choir instead, and also for affirming the areas of music where I showed true promise. I thank my college voice teachers and choral conductors J. P. Jardine and Jerry Warren; my college advisor Richard Shadinger; my piano teachers Anne Scott and Richard Lamar; and graduate school choral conductors Richard Lin and Don Hustad; who each built upon the foundation laid by my early childhood teachers, and who took special interest and time to be a mentor in my emerging interest in music as a career. I also thank my college and graduate school peers, Patricia Caldwell, Gary Stewart, Lois Johnson, Tim Waugh, Keith Guyton, Gary Kirksey, Craig Hodges, Paul Richardson, Bill Clemmons, and others, for freely sharing what they were learning and experiencing in our shared musical settings.

I thank my daughter Emma and wife Jane for their years of understanding of what I was trying to do as an artist, for attending every possible recital and concert, and for their discernment in recent years regarding what the artist needs, does not need, and the importance of timing in the ongoing learning process.

Finally, I thank my protégés for their interest and trust.

ARIOSO

Mentoring Defined

To the world, you may just be somebody. But to somebody, you just might be the world.

—author unknown

The academic study in the psychosocial arena of mentor and protégé is in relatively early stages, considering the phenomenon has taken place, in one form or another, since before Socrates passed on to Plato his open-ended mode of asking questions as a pedagogical tool.

The source of the word *mentor* dates back to the proper name of a friend of Odysseus, Mentor, who was charged with educating Odysseus' son. This places the origin of the concept of mentoring in ancient Greek literature. Even with this noble history, the formal study of mentoring as a learning process within a social setting is relatively new to research.

Scholarship conducted over the last two decades has focused on the goal of defining the process of mentoring. A survey of this research, and the various definitions captured by those seriously studying this field, has led to a distillation of terms used throughout *Mentoring in the Ensemble Arts*. These terms and definitions offer an outline as well as an overview of the intentions and desirable outcomes of mentor and protégé.

This book has intentionally veered away from two styles of presentation, although at every turn it has been tempting to take these two typically good approaches. The first involves citing and quoting research studies and journals seeking to quantify and qualify the terms and psychosocial approaches to the topic of mentoring. These studies have informed the content of this volume and will be referenced and applied throughout to the ensemble arts, but the "name dropping" will be held to a minimum. The second involves providing a series of lists, "how-tos," forms, and other systematic guides to the mentoring process. Lists and steps will appear eventually, when appropriate for reflection and guidance, but this book is not intended to be a step-by-step field guide for the mentor and protégé.

Mentoring in the Ensemble Arts seeks to apply the research and lessons gained in the formal study of the mentoring process to the musical ensemble setting, and does not attempt to further probe the scholarly study of this emerging field. From articles that lament theory-driven research, to articles presenting the findings of hundreds of mentoring studies, the following definitions offer what has been explored and applied to the mentor–protégé environment.

While the terms and definitions used throughout this book will guide the application of mentoring to the ensemble setting, the various "thought experiments" offered for reflection and the extracts from formal studies of specific areas of research aim to bring clear focus to the potential of the ensemble as an environment for developing mentor–protégé relationships.

A comprehensive study of the various definitions of mentoring accumulated by Bozeman and Feeney (*Toward a Useful Theory of Mentoring*) is reflected in the definitions, analysis, and commentary. The analysis of their findings is intended to bring the topic, the terms, and the definitions of mentoring into strong focus for extended reflection toward application for potential conductor-mentors and ensemble member protégés.

In a study conducted by Smith, Howard, and Harrington, the term "mentor" refers to "a more senior person who takes an interest in sponsorship of the career of a more junior person." (p. 33) Tepper further describes the mentoring relationships as existing in order to "facilitate junior colleagues' (protégés') professional development and career progress." (p. 1191)

The following definition is the most comprehensive and all encompassing of those found in serious scholarship on the subject of mentors:

Definition of Mentoring:

Mentoring:
a process for the informal transmission of knowledge, social capital, and psychosocial support perceived by the recipient as relevant to work, career, or professional development; mentoring entails informal communication, usually face-to-face and during a sustained period of time, between a person who is perceived to have greater relevant knowledge, wisdom, or experience (the mentor) and a person who is perceived to have less (the protégé).
(Bozeman and Feeney, p. 731)

This definition of mentoring inserts key descriptors, such as "process," "social," and "face-to-face," as well as outcomes desired, such as "transmission of knowledge," "psychosocial support," and "professional development." This definition further describes the mentor as a person with "greater relevant knowledge, wisdom, or experience" and the protégé who is less experienced, and offers the environment of their relationship as "informal." A key element in this definition relevant to the conductor and ensemble, is the temporal parameter of a "sustained period of time," which is a given application condition of the ensemble rehearsal setting.

In two additional studies, the following short definitions add the keyword "developmental," offering a clue to the organic nature of the organizational members involved in the mentoring relationship. Bozionelos states, "Mentoring is defined as a developmental relationship that involves organizational members of unequal status or, less frequently, peers." (p. 25) McManus and Russell add, "Mentoring is a developmental relationship typically occurring between senior and junior individuals in organizations." (p. 145)

The length of the mentoring relationship is defined as "an intense long-term relationship" in a study conducted by Eby and Allen, further qualifying the earlier designation of the mentoring term as a "sustained period of time." (p. 146) Once again, the nature of the ensemble situation sets up both the passive long-term relationship between conductor and protégé, as well as the sustained period of time in which they work together.

In a pragmatic definition focusing on the deliverables for the protégé in the mentoring relationship, Kram and Isabella state, "Mentors provide young adults with career-enhancing functions, such as sponsorship, coaching, facilitating exposure and visibility, and offering challenging work or protection, all of which help the younger person to establish a role in the organization, learn the ropes, and prepare for advancement." (p. 111) The emphasis upon career enhancement and advancement within an organization offer a glimpse at the desired outcomes of an intentional mentoring relationship.

Noe states that the mentor "is usually a senior, experienced employee who serves as a role model, provides support, direction, and feedback to the younger employee regarding career plans and inter-personal development, and increases the visibility of the protégé to decision-makers in the organization who may influence career opportunities." (p. 458)

Zey continues this line of thought by stating, "A mentor is a person who oversees the career and development of another person, usually junior, through teaching, counseling, providing psychological support, protecting, and at times promoting or sponsoring. The mentor may perform any or all of the above functions during the mentor relationship." (p. 7) Introduced in these definitions is the concept of the mentor as role model, and the role model's contribution to the protégé's "psychological support," a key element in the mentoring relationship. An interesting concept added to this definition is the word "protect," which is derived from the French verb *protéger*, "to protect."

The word "committed" appears in some definitions of the mentoring process. Ragins states: "Traditionally, mentors are defined as individuals with advanced experience and knowledge who are committed to providing upward mobility and support to protégés' careers." (p. 484) The use of the word "committed" gives ownership and added power to the definition; it is again found in a study by Singh, Bains, and Vinnicombe, where mentors are described as "individuals with advanced experience and knowledge who are committed to providing upward support and mobility to their protégés' careers." (p. 391) This implies that becoming a mentor is something of a calling to individuals who take on this task, and who remain intentionally engaged in the task of advancing the protégé's career goals.

Throughout *Mentoring in the Ensemble Arts*, the conductor of an ensemble will be the mentor focus. Various formal mentoring studies refer to the mentor as supervisor, or in other cases, as an influential person in the work environment. Ragins, Cotton, and Miller define the mentor as one that is generally "… a higher-ranking, influential individual in your work environment who has advanced experience and knowledge…" They also state that the mentor "may or may not be in your organization and s/he may or may not be your immediate supervisor." (p. 1182) This definition expands the boundaries of mentoring beyond the same organization and beyond the parameter of one's supervisor.

It is the underlying assumption that the mentoring environment will result in the positive transformation of the protégé. This transformation, along with accompanying added confidence, will result in the transmission of skills and knowledge from mentor to protégé. In addition, this transformation will include the sharing of values from mentor to protégé. In their study of this topic, Scandura and Schriesheim stated the following:

> We conceptualized supervisory mentoring as a transformational activity involving a mutual commitment by mentor and protégé to the latter's long-term development, as a personal, extra organizational

> investment in the protégé by the mentor, and as the changing of the protégé by the mentor, accomplished by the sharing of values, knowledge, experience, and so forth. (p. 1589)

The idea that the mentor–protégé development work is "extra organizational" and an "investment" suggests an informal relationship outside the realm of requirement of a classroom or organization. Such a setting could ably describe the ensemble setting as shared between conductor and ensemble member.

Throughout this book, formal and informal mentoring styles are assumed to exist side by side. A more formal type of relationship could be established between mentor and protégé when vocation or career is introduced into the equation; simultaneously, informal mentoring may take place in a passive environment.

More and more organizations officially recognize the need for and importance of mentoring, and more and more individuals seek to develop their own personal learning communities. Young and Perrewe point out that formal levels of mentoring are becoming more prevalent in the socialization and career development of many professionals. (p. 611)

These definitions and reflections offer the terms and context on which the content of *Mentoring in the Ensemble Arts* is based, and they provide a framework for the applications made to the relationship between the conductor and certain ensemble members. Clearly, most of the terms used to define the relationship between mentor and protégé exist quite naturally in the ensemble environment and take place passively on a routine basis between conductor and ensemble members. The purpose here is to bring into clear focus the elements of the passive mentor–protégé relationship within the environment of the musical ensemble. The intent is to help the conductor-mentor realize the full potential of this helpful relationship, and to assist the protégé in fulfilling all the possible beneficial outcomes within this environment.

When informal mentoring develops toward the concept of intentional mentoring, additional considerations as well as formal steps and procedures will be explored to help bring the mentor-protégé relationship into a more systematic and structured mentoring process.

The Renaissance Bottega

One's mind, once stretched by a new idea never regains its original dimensions.

—Oliver Wendell Holmes

In the mid-1460s the teenage Leonardo da Vinci left his namesake home of Vinci, Italy, for Florence, where he was apprenticed to the sculptor Andrea del Verrocchio. According to Vasari, it was Leonardo's father who arranged the apprenticeship.

The conventional age to begin apprenticeship in Leonardo's time was around thirteen or fourteen. Michelangelo and Botticini entered apprenticeship at the age of 13; Caravaggio at 11; Cellini at 15. In Leonardo's case this means he entered Verrocchio's studio in about 1466.

Florence in the mid-1460s was a city of some 50,000 people. In Leonardo's day, the word in use for the environment he entered for artistic mentoring was *bottega*, which simply means a shop, or workshop. Further, the bottega was a community of learners.

It was not unusual for an apprentice to adopt his master's name and then become his "son" within the "family" of artisans. Andrea Verrocchio was about thirty when he became Leonardo's master and artistic mentor. Andrea was clearly Leonardo's senior, both in age and artistic experience.

While serving as a junior worker in the studio, and perhaps also as a model, Leonardo was also a *discepolo* (pupil), receiving specific instruction from the *maestro* (teacher) Andrea. A contract drawn up in 1467 states that the teacher will undertake to teach his pupil "the principle of a plane, with lines drawn according to my method," and how to "put figures on the said plane" and how to "place objects there, as namely a chair or a bench or a house," how to "represent a man's head in foreshortening in isometric rendering," and the system of "drawing a body." These were the essential basic lessons for the protégé. (Nicholl, p. 77).

Therefore, broadly speaking, the protégé Leonardo would learn the techniques of perspective and figure drawing. The mentor also promised to "keep him with paper in his hand" and to "provide him with models." These models would be the master's own drawings, real objects, as well as human models. The protégé spent much time copying from the mentor's model book.

These descriptions give us a picture of Leonardo da Vinci the protégé. After he left the bottega, we know something of his ongoing mentoring due to his well-established processes of learning and observation. Leonardo kept journals we call notebooks and fortunately, these notebooks have been preserved.

We learn from the mature Leonardo, who later in life becomes a mentor, by his constant posing of the question *perche?* or *why?* We hear the following lesson from his writing: "Many wish to learn how to draw, and enjoy drawing, but do not have a true aptitude for it. This is shown by their lack of perseverance, like boys who draw everything in a hurry, never finishing or shadowing…" (Nicholl, p. 77)

The mature Leonardo had asked and answered the question *why?* for his own discipline and life, passing along his lessons through his art, inventions, and writing.

Thought Experiment

Leonardo's artistic and professional transformation took on formal dimensions as he moved from the home and family environment to the artistic bottega. The bottega, or workshop, was a stimulating learning and working environment, filled with the tools and sensations of interest to the aspiring protégé-artist.

Think of the first time you experienced a personal "bottega" in the form of a musical ensemble or group musical experience. Think about the images and experiences, both musical and extra-musical, which captured your imagination within that environment.

- What characteristics do you recall of your early leaders?
- What characteristics do you recall of your early conductors?
- What characteristics do you recall of influential peers within this environment.
- Do any of these characteristics constitute what you might call mentoring?

Did any of the following take place?

- Did you feel acceptance and a sense of belonging?
- Did you feel a sense of calling or destiny within the ensemble?
- Did you feel encouragement and affirmation?
- Where did these feelings come from and who was responsible for them?
- Where did such feelings, or lack of such feelings, lead you?
- What do you wish could have been added to those early experiences?

Our Early Mentors

Most people would rather give than get affection.
—Aristotle

Traditionally, the incubator for mentoring in all aspects of life has been the family unit: from learning basic survival, how to communicate, how to relate to others, to learning the tools and techniques of a trade toward ongoing sustenance—whether the arena was a cave, a rural outpost, a medieval village, or a modern home.

As Pipher puts it: "Families are ancient institutions. Since humans crossed the savannas in search of food, our families have been unique." She continues, "We are born helpless and dependent, and after birth our brains continue to grow. Homo sapiens need families to survive." (Pipher, p. 4)

The family was and has been the heart of learning what it means to belong to a social organization, and how to perpetuate a social order. If the family was functional, society progressed as it had in the past. If the family was dysfunctional, new elements entered into the social fabric in the evolutionary chain.

The family model is good at creating allegiance to the family structure, but unless mentoring turned to the larger community, allegiance and focus remained only with the family. As families gathered with other families in societal settings, clans protected clans for the sake of perpetuating families within a larger community. The clan further developed the abilities of the individual outside the influence of the immediate family.

As civilized communities developed, the family and clan system of mentoring melded into institutions formed to broaden the exclusive allegiance to family structure, and expanded the contribution to the goals of the community. Historically, the church and school augmented the process of *generativity*. (See the section on Generativity on page 67 for further explanation.)

In some religious communities, authorities placed children and youth into living groups according to age and gender, and later marital status. As is true of most religious traditions, intentional communities developed in order to perpetuate continuing plausibility structures of those religious groups. Sanctioned actions and traditions were passed along, mentors to protégés, in order to perpetuate community and social structure.

Alternatively, a person might be moved outside the family structure and, rather than mentoring in a religious community, the person learned a trade from a guild or other trade group as an apprentice as was the case in the Italian bottega. The process of apprenticeship was a necessary step in earlier times, and an absolute requirement in the arts.

Throughout the literature of every culture, fictional mentors have entered the imagination of writers and storytellers, passing along the lessons of life through characters of fantasy, myth, legend (for example, Merlin to young King Arthur), heroics, and even the most ordinary of individuals. The key to their place in the collective imagination is that they have traveled the road before us and are willing to tell us what lies ahead.

Institutes and academies developed in order to augment all of these social structures and conduits of experience for the further refinement of knowledge and skills. Through the development of all of these plausibility structures, there has always been a place for the relationship of mentor and protégé, however it may have developed, and whatever form the mentoring process may have taken.

The musical ensemble exists first and foremost as a musical instrument. Inevitably, and by definition, a social structure is formed when groups of musicians gather together. Professional, amateur, pro-am, trained, being trained—the ensemble unit shares characteristics with the family, clan, tribe, apprentice studio, church, and school. The conductor is the leader that passes on the lessons and structures to the ensemble.

Thought Experiment

In the healthy family structure, the parents, first and foremost, provide protection for the baby and young child, continuing until the child is on his or her own. In this context, protection means safety from physical and emotional harm.

In the context of the musical ensemble, protection does not conjure the same images of safety. However, protection can still be applied to the mentoring relationship.

Reflect on how to apply the concept of protection within the setting of the musical ensemble:

- Protection related to basic musicianship?
- Protection related to working in a social structure such as an ensemble?
- Protection related to physical and emotional issues connected to performance?
- Protection related to the lessons advanced in rehearsal and performance?
- Protection related to vocation and career?

The "Why?" of Mentoring

I live in that solitude which is painful in youth, but delicious in the years of maturity.

—Albert Einstein

No matter the discipline, the fine commitment, the fine skill, and the fine art of mentoring has more to do with the "why" of what it is we do when we perform than the when, what, where, or even the significant "how" we perform our craft and art. "Why?" drives us, in Leonardo's words, to "persevere" in a discipline.

When we explore the question of "why" we do what we do, we are looking into the philosophical, psychological, and moral realms of values, motivation, ethics, and fundamental reasons for being.

The "what" and "how" of the musical discipline will undoubtedly be a part of the experience, and on many occasions, the tools and skills of the trade will form much of the vocabulary and conversation of the relationship between mentor and protégé. Once again, Leonardo identifies "aptitude" as necessary for the pursuit of a discipline. The "why" of a discipline is the shared experience between protégé and mentor that drives the lifelong pursuit of dedication to the work.

There is no question that the answers and skills needed in the quest of how we do our work, when we do it, where we do it, and how we do it, are fundamentally significant as a person seeks to build a successful career. As musicians, we work with a highly codified and scientific language that must be mastered in order to convey musical ideas and to learn, interpret, and perform the ideas of others. Time and context demonstrate over and over that there are best practices, better ways, and better times and settings in which to do our work as performers. The refined skills and expertise required to teach and perform, along with desire, passion, and innate talent, are necessary components of a lifelong pursuit for any person choosing to make a vocation in the musical arts.

It is the "why" we do what we do, however, that will become the pursuit that may be most perplexing to us, those with whom we work, and those we work to influence. Talent and hard work produce amazing results in all fields of inquiry, but the "why" question is deeply personal and will continue to be adjusted in every individual throughout life. It is the question "why" that brings the relationship between protégé and mentor into sharpest focus.

The two terms of primary importance in this book are the terms *mentor* and *protégé*. Of the many titles a person already carries through life, the terms mentor and protégé may come and go, active when the role is formally engaged, and passive when informally engaged.

In the context of this exploration, a mentor is a person that brings informed, experienced application and wisdom to a skill set that is of mutual concern to another person in the same field of inquiry. As surveyed in our introductory definitions, the word *mentor* has been used to define a temporary or long-term relationship, informal or formal, in which a person of experience and advanced knowledge assists a less experienced or less knowledgeable person, the protégé.

A protégé is a person that willingly seeks informed, experienced application and wisdom from another person. We use this noun to refer to one who is protected or trained, or whose career is furthered by a person of experience, prominence, or influence. However, the protégé also "protects" the skills and lessons learned from the mentor as the protégé moves on into life and into a career. In earlier times, protection was no doubt applicable to the relationship, and in the days of apprenticeships, training in a skill or art can be easily understood within a protective environment, and within an environment that would protect trade secrets and techniques. Today, the image of protecting is more easily used as a metaphor for the competitive workplace, or for the protégé's need for psychosocial support, career advancement, and sponsorship. However, it is because of this meaning, "to protect," that I prefer to use the term protégé to the synonymous term *mentee*, which is simply derived from the Greek proper name Mentor.

Mentoring refers to a process, generally informal, in which experience and knowledge is transferred from mentor to protégé.

These traits are outlined in the comprehensive definition described by Bozeman and Feeney:

> Mentoring is a process for the informal transmission of knowledge, social capital, and the psychosocial support perceived by the recipient as relevant to work, career, or professional development; mentoring entails informal communication, usually face-to-face and during a sustained period of time, between a person who is perceived to have greater relevant knowledge, wisdom, or experience (the mentor) and a person who is perceived to have less (the protégé). (p. 731)

Kram (1985) noted that mentoring involves an intense relationship whereby a senior or more experienced person (the mentor) provides two functions for a junior person (the protégé); one function being advice or modeling about career development behaviors, and the second function being personal support, especially psychosocial support.

In the context of ensemble rehearsal and performance, the conductor models technical behaviors, while simultaneously interpreting and motivating a diverse group of individuals. Mentoring takes place under these conditions, although the form it takes falls outside most conventional definitions. A similar dynamic takes place in a more limited focus through team sports and other group situations.

This symbiotic relationship between mentor and protégé continues for a period of time, defined either by mutual understanding, ongoing proximity, or until the relationship has run its natural course. A protégé and mentor may retain their titles within the relationship for the duration of a particular lesson, season, or throughout life. The use of the term, after the process has run its course, is generally considered a professional acknowledgment. The statements "she is my mentor," or "he was my mentor" may indicate temporary situations, or designate lifelong relationships, and may actually be saying the same thing during and after the process has come to formal completion.

Mentoring in the Ensemble Arts addresses the mentor–protégé relationship unique to the musical arts, and particularly to the area of musical ensembles. In this context, the relationship is one between ensemble member as protégé, and ensemble conductor as mentor.

Ensemble members look to the conductor of the performing group for a variety of leadership questions. In a very practical way, ensemble members watch the conductor for the meter and tempo of a musical composition. Singers and players look to the conductor for entrances and cut offs within a piece of music. Musicians look to the conductor for interpretive cues, such as musical dynamics, tempo variations, and the character of the music being performed. These are the pragmatic functions of the conductor in the rehearsal and performance arena that serve the needs of the musical score. The decisions a conductor makes in these particular areas will be informed by years of study of formal disciplines such as music theory, musical form, historical performance practice, music psychology, acoustics, vocal, keyboard, and instrumental technique, and span the gamut of intellectual and emotional reflections that bring music to life.

With all of that said, there is yet another area the protégé may be looking to the mentor for lessons, and that the mentor may wish to convey to a protégé. This area is embodied in the question of "why": "Why I chose this music?"; "Why I chose this profession?"; "Why I chose this program?"; "Why I conceived this tour?"; "Why this tempo for this piece of music?"; and the *whys?* go on and on.

Significantly, the ensemble conductor interprets the music being performed by the ensemble, drawing from the experience of his or her life. These experiences come through social interaction, formal education, discretionary reading, travel, and the myriad events in life. These experiences find their way into the musical interpretation a conductor gives to the ensemble by means of metaphor, story, analogy, and every communication tool at the disposal of the conductor. Interpretation is directly connected to the technical instruction that flows from conductor to ensemble.

For the mentor, the desire to pass on information and life experiences is a part of generativity—contributing to the good of the profession and to the good of another individual. For the protégé, the desire to learn from a skilled, insightful, and experienced individual is a natural part of maturation. Whether acknowledged or unacknowledged, formal or passive, this flow takes place in every ensemble rehearsal between conductor and ensemble musician.

Thought Experiment

If you could create a "professional will," articulating exactly what you would like to contribute to sustaining the life of your musical profession, based on the professional assets you have accumulated throughout life and the professional inheritance you have acquired, what would you place on such a list?

- What professional concepts and items have you inherited that you would like to pass on to others?
- What professional assets have you acquired through your hard work and experience?
- What professional axioms and quotes have you acquired that you would like orally transmitted to others?
- If you could dispose of any "toxic" professional assets, what would they be?
- If you were choosing the bank or monetary equivalent of safekeeping your desirable professional assets, what would that professional investment instrument be?

A Personal Word

To exist is to change, to change is to mature, to mature is to go on creating oneself endlessly.

—Henri Bergson

The lasting, formational influences on our lives begin before infancy, grow through childhood and adolescence, and continue for as long as we recognize the impact others have on our thinking and our behavior. While many of the influences of our early years may fade in our memories, assuming the noble mentoring title of "mom," "dad," "teacher," or "friend," it is likely that later mentors who devote the time and energy to our development are the ones that we remember and reference more regularly as "mentor" throughout life. Our early mentors fade into those lifelong endearing terms, while our adult mentors are usually named by name. They are all mentors, but we have reserved a different place for them in the acknowledgment of our development. At least, that is true in my life.

When one of my primary life and career mentors, Don Hustad, retired and moved to a location closer to his children and grandchildren in his later years, this giant in my career made a point of sending some of the physical reminders of his work and craft to his protégés. It was a personal and extraordinarily meaningful gesture on his part. The personal items from his life's work arrived without a note of explanation, or even a signature—none was needed. The message was clear and self-apparent. This mentor knew I would know the meaning of this gift, and he also knew I had no practical need for it. He knew it was a symbolic gesture, as he continued to mentor.

In my case, this symbol took the form of the leather attaché satchel he had carried to work throughout my graduate school experience, and certainly before and after my time with him. It was a satchel that had contained all of the scores we had studied and performed together in ensemble settings. It was the satchel that had held my doctoral dissertation and its many drafts and corrections. It was the satchel that had contained my research papers and score analysis sheets. And of course, it contained the drafts of letters that contained ideas and arrangements and conditions that were a part of his career and influence.

And for a period of time, in that satchel, his musical scores and my musical scores were transported together; his writings mingled with mine; his editorial work nested side by side with mine; his documents and letters and mine shared the same place. This, of course, was a metaphor for the knowledge, wisdom, musical, and life lessons that had made their way from mentor to protégé.

All of that work, and the lessons gained from the academy and performance hall, have now made their mark in publication and performance, and in their influence on other thinkers. What remained after the passing of the years was that satchel, which marked a time when mentor and protégé connected, first informally and then formally.

The leather of the satchel showed the wear of the many years of his career. The leather, like my career, had been shaped by the materials inside the case. The wear on the outside of the case had come from transporting the material to every important place in the world my mentor had lectured and performed. In the early years of my career, I retraced many of those steps myself, following in my mentor's footsteps. For the mentor and protégé, this is all perfectly natural.

But at this point, of all the characteristics represented by this symbol of what my mentor had given to me in the later years, it is the handle of the satchel that means the most to me. It was *his hand* that held that handle every working day of his life. The shape of that handle came from the shape of his hand bearing the weight of the material inside the satchel. That part of the case reminds me of what his hand, and the material he introduced to me, has done to guide and weight my life and career.

The satchel sits beside my desk today as a visual reminder of who I am and where I came from. For me, it also serves as a reminder of my own responsibility toward helping others find their voice. Since receiving this iconic gift from my career mentor, I have used it occasionally to carry the essays, discs, letters, documents, and images that I had gathered for the publication of a Festschrift (a publication honoring a respected person in academia) in my mentor's honor. In a personal way, it seemed important to me to bring this case full circle to honor the life of the mentor who had given so much to so many protégés.

The desire and ability to help another individual refine a skill set or perpetuate the good in one's vocational pursuit, is most likely symptomatic of the greater desire to help another individual find purpose and happiness in life. Research demonstrates that the desire to mentor another individual is a strong indicator of the ultimate success of a mentor–protégé experience and relationship.

While always aware of the external realities that bear upon work and home life, ultimately, a protégé is looking to a mentor to help deal with life beyond external circumstances. It is tempting for a protégé to simply try to parrot the so-called "secrets" of a mentor's success. However, humans are not destined to be clones, and the protégé will deal with a completely different set of life circumstances than did the mentor. Those secrets of a mentor's success should help provide something of a directional compass, no matter the circumstances.

The pursuit of happiness, coupled with vocational success, is both easier and harder that it would seem. As Mihály Csíkszentmihályi states, "achieving control over experience requires a drastic change in attitude about what is important and what is not." (p. 16)

The greatest lessons for which a mentor can provide guidance reside in this pursuit of what is, and what is not, important.

Thought Experiment

Mentors and protégés come along at different times and stages in our personal development and varied environmental settings. Different levels of education, different vocational directions, different family situations, and different living locations and conditions all elicit thoughts of different environments and conditions for a variety of mentoring situations.

Reflect on times you have been a mentor and times you have been a protégé in each of the following life situations:

- Family Environment
- Educational Environment
- Vocational Environment
- Social and Recreational Environment
- Citizenship Environment

In each of these environments, reflect on traits that were most important in your role as mentor and which lessons were most important for you as protégé.

In each of the environments listed above, recall an "a-ha" moment, an epiphany, or a moment or situation when you uncovered an unrecognized talent, skill possibility, or ability. Who helped prompt that moment? How did this discovery develop?

Our Reason for Being

A mature person is one who does not think only in absolutes, who is able to be objective even when deeply stirred emotionally, who has learned that there is both good and bad in all people and all things, and who walks humbly and deals charitably.

—Eleanor Roosevelt

The formal reason for being a part of any musical ensemble is to make beautiful musical sounds, to afford ensemble musicians the opportunity for expression and satisfaction in rehearsal, and if rehearsals lead to performance, to share such expression and satisfaction with a listening audience. In these settings, ensemble members learn from both the conductor and from other musicians in the ensemble.

The range of expression for an ensemble runs the gamut from exploring historically meaningful compositions, to reading through newly composed works, to improvising new sounds and musical ideas in the moment. Ensembles making these expressions range in size from a very small group, to groups with a hundred or more musicians.

In most ensemble settings, a single conductor directs the course of the group. This person functions as organizer, interpreter, teacher, administrator, and motivator. In each of these areas, the success of the conductor will be measured to some degree in terms of his or her success in musical and administrative leadership, as well as in the ability to motivate others to action.

The capable conductor has an allegiance first and foremost to the musical score and the intentions of the composer or arranger. The actualization of this is the task to which the conductor is dedicated—all the conductor's training and experience is at the service of the musical score. To this end, the conductor's ability as teacher, interpreter, motivator, and leader are on full display to the ensemble and to the listening public. Due to the visible and public nature of the conductor's work, the successful conductor's leadership role usually does not end with these musical tasks.

The conductor also works to secure an ensemble's ongoing sustainability, which involves work in the areas of recruitment, financial development, community relations, other administrative duties, and the all-important area of vision. Even when these duties are enhanced and assisted by the work of a board, artistic committee, or other administrative body, the conductor is the one person standing up and out front, both in rehearsal and performance, in full view of everyone: performer and audience. So while there may be hundreds of audience members, dozens of ensemble members, or several board members, there is only one conductor, and all eyes eventually fall on that person for leadership and modeling.

The purpose of *Mentoring in the Ensemble Arts* is to explore the additional role served by the conductor as mentor. Research has demonstrated that one in four volunteer ensemble members continue in an ensemble because of their interest in working with the conductor. The mentoring role to various members of the ensemble is often silent and often passive. Nevertheless, the role of conductor as mentor is taking place simultaneously with other musical and administrative tasks outlined above. And while an ever-developing and ever-refining pedagogy continues to define the technical aspects of individual and group musical performance, little, if any, attention has been given to the mentoring that takes place within the ensemble environment between conductor and performer.

Due to the informal and passive development of the mentoring process that grows naturally in the rehearsal environment, formal procedures and systems are rarely, if ever, put into place to assist a mentor and protégé in this important developmental process.

The concept of a "formal mentor" in the ensemble rehearsal situation may, by definition, be something of an oxymoron. However, such systems have indeed been formalized in many other traditional educational environments, business environments, and other settings where expertise and networks are valued, in addition to methodological systems of formal training and certification. And whether informal and passive, or formal and intentional, the fact that this mentor–protégé exchange is taking place within the ensemble environment is far too significant in the life of the conductor and ensemble member to be taken for granted.

The research and literature on the subject of mentoring suggests that most mentor–protégé relationships involve informal social exchange, even when programs have been systematized or otherwise formalized. The terms "informal" and "formal" are used in this context primarily to distinguish between "unacknowledged" mentoring and "acknowledged" mentoring.

While the experience of a protégé observing the model and gaining personal inspiration in an ensemble may not be celebrated to the same degree as the audible aspect of rehearsing and performing music, nevertheless, a powerful mentoring activity is indeed taking place in these settings with certain individuals. And significantly, in some instances, the mentoring process may move from informal to formal in the ensemble setting as a protégé is identified and the process takes on formal characteristics.

As Executive Director of the American Choral Directors Association and observer of hundreds of conductors and ensembles, I have been witness over and over to the quite natural development of the mentor–protégé relationship within the ensemble setting. More significantly, however, interviews and conversations with hundreds of conductors and ensemble members has led me to realize that the development within the ensemble setting toward a mentor–protégé relationship, while a common occurrence, is still under analyzed and lacking in helpful analysis, guidelines, suggestions, and protective elements for both protégé and mentor.

The first step in a more intentional investigation of the mentor–protégé relationship within the musical ensemble environment is to acknowledge the strong presence of this ongoing activity. This book is written to assist and inform acknowledged mentoring and its stages of growth within the musical ensemble, as well as to inform mentoring that takes place within the regular routine and process of rehearsal and performance.

The process defined in the following pages explores territory not defined by a traditional classroom, course syllabi, or the more codified and recognized teacher–student role in the academy. The process does not assume the boundaries of a school term, semester, or degree program, but rather, explores the more open territory where grades and credentials are not of primary concern. The fact is, while many ensembles reside within academic settings, equal or greater numbers of ensembles exist outside the parameter of the academy.

The primary subject explored in this book is the concept of generativity—the process of passing lessons along from one person to another, as well as the process of assisting in the advancement of the life success of another individual. In the context of a musical rehearsal and performance environment, these lessons certainly include the lessons of expertise and skill within the conducting and rehearsal/performance discipline. Significantly, however, in addition to these musical lessons, the teaching of values and ethics, vocational work style, life priorities, relationships, networking, and other lessons embodied by the director, and applied and viewed in and around the ensemble environment, constitute additional lessons of vocational and personal interest to the protégé.

The level of mentoring will vary widely depending on whether or not the conductor embraces the mentoring role, and whether or not the process is acknowledged, unacknowledged, passive, active, informal, formal, or structured. However, the dynamics of the environment and the outlook of ensemble members remain consistent. Mentoring is taking place and lessons are being observed and learned; both career lessons and life lessons.

Thought Experiment

The rehearsal has its unique opportunities for encounter between conductor and ensemble member, and the performance also has its unique opportunities for encounter. Thinking through your rehearsal process and performance experience, consider the following list of personal encounter moments between conductor and ensemble members:

- Initial contact with ensemble member.
- Audition or interview.
- Acceptance into ensemble.
- Rehearsal encounters.
- Performance encounters.

Now consider your unique rehearsal and performance routines and procedures and add them to the above list. Reviewing the list, reflect on the many and varied ways the conductor interacts with ensemble performers in each of these encounters with an eye toward mentorship.

Although the conductor will rarely analyze social encounters with the ensemble members with attention toward the mentor–protégé environment, such an analysis might nonetheless reveal the small but important moments of opportunity and teachable moments for both mentor and protégé.

ARIA

LISTENING FOR THE VOICE
Framing the Mentoring Environment

What we have done for ourselves alone dies with us. What we have done for others and the world remains and is immortal.
—Albert Pine

In order to frame this exploration of the mentor-protégé environment, the following two Thought Experiments will help you to visualize rehearsal situations typical of those that occur in an ensemble setting.

The following examples are fictional but are comprised of details that have occurred in many individual examples throughout my experience as a conductor and throughout my observation of conductors. These two scenarios are offered to assist the reader in the identification of a setting in which the mentor-protégé relationship develops in the rehearsal environment.

Thought Experiment

Martin conducts a community ensemble that has enjoyed a long history in his region. The performances of this ensemble are widely recognized as part of the cultural landscape of the community. He is only the most recent in a list of fine conductors that have been on the podium as artistic director and leader. Like many conductors, Martin balances his conducting of the ensemble with other responsibilities and it is clear that his expertise and skill set contribute to his excellent reputation as well as to the ongoing vitality of the ensemble. The community praises his artistic leadership for innovative programming, energetic performances by his musicians, sensitive musicianship, and for the ensemble's cultural contribution to the region.

Kate is a recent addition to the ensemble, joining the group with an impressive background in performance. Kate has received much affirmation as a solo performer and continues to study with enthusiasm and delight in musical performance. Lately Kate has been thinking about the future and about the many possibilities for applying and expressing the musical interest and vocational satisfaction she experiences in music and musical performance. Kate enjoys performing for Martin and she knows that Martin has a bank of knowledge that she can barely tap in the usual rehearsal setting.

Martin has noticed a spark in Kate and knows that Kate's talent is exceptional. He looks for opportunities to showcase Kate as a soloist and provides leadership opportunities for her in the ensemble; Kate is grateful to have these experiences and the opportunity to perform in this ensemble under Martin's leadership. Kate knows that the experience she gains as a member of this ensemble is exceptional and she values the time she spends in this musical environment.

Thought Experiment

Sara has been conductor of the Chorale for several years and enjoys a strong reputation that she built over time for fine performances and enthusiastic participation by ensemble performers. Performers return to the ensemble every year and new members regularly join the ensemble as needed. Sara's excellent musicianship and strong work ethic have earned her much recognition in the community, and her colleagues respect her as a collaborator. She has demonstrated success in balancing the challenges of sustaining an ensemble in terms of both internal demands and external obstacles. All the while, she continues to motivate performers and excite audiences.

James has been a performing member of Sara's Chorale for two years; over that time he has noticed how much he has enjoyed his work with the ensemble and how much he has learned from Sara. His learning began naturally with Sara introducing and teaching new performing material to the ensemble; over time, Sara's influence extended into other areas of learning and growth. James found himself applying with success techniques he had learned earlier to new material. He found himself appropriating terms and insights he had learned within the ensemble experience, and he even found himself taking on new musical challenges by thinking about what Sara might say about a similar challenge encountered in the past.

Sara is obviously comfortable with her skills and she demonstrates dedication to lifelong learning and personal growth. James is a talented performer but is only beginning to develop his career and base of experience. Knowing that Sara is both a totally engaged professional as well as an approachable person, James has determined that there is much about Sara's superior abilities and obvious success that he would like to eventually model in his career. After determining that Sara possesses skills and personal traits that he thinks would make him a better musician and leader, James decides to ask Sara if she would enter into a mentoring relationship with him.

Important Questions About Mentoring—The following questions, which surface as a result of engaging in the above two Thought Experiments, help to frame the analysis of the mentor–protégé relationship in the chapters that follow. These questions are meant to be rhetorical in order to raise important elements, which the formal and informal activity of mentoring contain. Reflection on these questions and answers will serve as preparation for the pages ahead.

- Is acknowledgment required for a mentoring relationship?
- Who is mentor and who is protégé?
- Must the mentor and the protégé respect one another?
- What part of knowledge transmission is "mentoring" and what part is not?
- What additional structure is necessary to help guide the mentor-protégé experience?
- When does the mentoring relationship begin and when does it end?
- Can groups mentor individuals?

Generativity

Maturity is that time when the mirrors in our mind turn to windows and instead of seeing the reflection of ourselves, we see others.

—author unknown

Generativity is the term coined by psychoanalyst Erik Erikson in 1950 to denote "a concern for establishing and guiding the next generation." This attribute formed the seventh stage in Erikson's theory of psychosocial development. The motivation for generativity is the desire of the individual to give back, to make a difference, to take care of another person, and/or to take care of the community. This process can be, and has been, expressed in countless ways, such as raising a child, correcting an abuse, writing a family history, choosing a vocation of service, starting a community watch program, mentoring another individual, and so on.

In this study, the process of generativity is the acknowledged imparting of proven techniques, knowledge, skills, and life lessons (including the "why" of the profession) from mentor to protégé, with the underlying belief that not only does the mentor share skills with the protégé but also the reasons for sharing the pursuit.

The mentor in this focus is the conductor and director of a musical ensemble. This mentor is clearly in a position of recognized leadership. As pointed out earlier, it is easy to know which person is the conductor—as a living metaphor to this study, it is the one standing up straight and facing the members of the ensemble for their undivided attention with his or her back to the audience. That very posture represents so much that is a part of the mentoring process—recognized leadership, acknowledged skills, artistic leader, administrative manager, professional humility, and other badges of leadership: knowledge, success, and accomplishment.

The immediate and apparent protégé in this focus could be defined potentially as the full body of performers making up the musical ensemble; however, the protégé that is truly the point of this study will be defined as those specific individuals looking to the conductor for more than tempo, entrances, cut-offs, and interpretation of the score. The protégé acknowledges the desire to learn personally from the mentor in a relationship of shared values and trust.

The protégé could be a specific individual that self-identifies to the conductor, or someone who continues in the ensemble as a passive protégé without specific acknowledgement. From time to time, and when appropriate, I will make a distinction between active and passive protégés in the ensemble relationship, which is a core aspect of the purpose of this book. At other times, assume that the two can be mutually inclusive.

In the Japanese language, this process is called *sedai-keisho-sei*. *Sedai* means "the generations." *Keisho* means "receive and put your stamp on." And *sei* means "the sense of." The spirit of the definition is that a person receives something from the past, creates something new out of it, and then passes it on to a future generation. This definition describes the process as embracing so much more than a set of skills. This creative flow is the process of mentoring and it takes place in every rehearsal experience with regard to both the immediate performance and the development of a protégé.

The Power of the Mentor

The unselfish effort to bring cheer to others will be the beginning of a happier life for ourselves.

—Helen Keller

The first challenge to the concept of generativity and the mentoring process is the question of motivation. The question, "what is the motivation for mentoring?" applies to both the mentor and the protégé. Similar to a friendship, both parties have to be interested in the process and the relationship, although this interest does not spring from the same source or desire as a friendship.

As the mentor approaches this work, it is helpful to first acknowledge the power base of a mentor and to commit to using this power constructively. While people respect power, they often distrust it because holders of power have been known to misuse it.

The best mentors commit to using any power they possess for the good of their protégés. It is therefore important to be honest about where such power resides.

The mentor is usually in some sort of supervisory capacity with the protégé or in some arena of influence related to the protégé's vocation or area of significant interest. Success, failure, and continuance are weights in the balance in one form or another. In an educational setting, these concerns exist in the area of grades or academic degrees; forms of professional recommendation, career advancement, and networking; and/or the passionate and engaged use of discretionary time and income. Endorsements, sponsorship, and attention by a mentor in these areas will influence the protégé's advancement or ongoing interest and participation.

In the ensemble arts, the mentoring might carry on in an academic setting, in a community setting, in a professional performance setting, or in a faith community setting; also, the context might be either professional or amateur.

The mentor has the power of affirmation within the professional field. A nod of approval or disapproval weighs heavily on the self-evaluation of the protégé seeking to learn from the mentor. This power of affirmation is the most important tool of influence at the mentor's disposal.

The knowledge, wisdom, judgment, and experience of the mentor are the reasons the protégé seeks the relationship in the first place, so the approval of the mentor is a powerful emotional element in the life of the protégé. The expression of this power can be as subtle as a nod or glance or as dramatic as public recognition and formal documentation. Furthermore, it is one of the most important areas of need for the protégé in a mentoring relationship.

The measure of a successful mentor-protégé relationship should conclude that in terms of both of these areas of power, supervision and affirmation, the mentor has positively propelled the life and work of the protégé and provided the mentor with the personal satisfaction that generativity has taken place.

The Conductor-Mentor and the Ensemble-Protégé

We make a living by what we get, we make a life by what we give.

—Winston Churchill

Who has ever said, "I want to be a mentor"? Who has ever had someone walk up to them and ask, "Would you be my mentor?" Perhaps once in a lifetime you might hear this, but it is unlikely. Yet as conductors we stand in front of groups in which this silent exchange takes place. While our singers gather to find and unify their musical voice, some are looking to find another voice—their inner voice and their artistic voice.

Randy Edwards, founder of the organization Youth Cue, an organization for teenagers with a choral focus, describes the mentor-protégé dynamic that exists in the youth choir rehearsal room. Edwards observes hundreds of conductors and their youth choirs every year and offers this insight into the mentoring dynamic:

> Teenagers sit in front of us each week whose foundation materials are dumped onto our podiums by default. The cement of teenagers' lives often piles up in an undefined blob right in front of us. The clarion call is to those of us

> who are willing to perform an urgent service, a ministry of molding, of smoothing, of soothing, of balancing and shaping. (p. 40)

Musical leaders might not be having the mentor-protégé conversation with their musicians as clearly and openly as stated in the questions "Will you mentor me?," or "Will you be my protégé?," but the call is certainly in front of the sensitive conductor, particularly when dealing with younger musicians.

According to recent research, for one out of four ensemble members the reason he or she is in, or remains in, the ensemble is the conductor. Certainly, this interest begins and centers around mutually held musical goals and purposes. However, it would be naïve to think that the ensemble member's ongoing attention would not grow to include other aspects of leadership offered by the seasoned musical conductor. The conductor will passively mentor those people throughout the rehearsal and performance process

Passive mentoring takes place in all of the rehearsals, performances, tours, and other situations where conductor is gathered with ensemble. In the routine activity of rehearsal, performing, and living out the life and work in front of the ensemble, mentoring is taking place. Everyone in the ensemble observes and a certain percentage of those observers are taking careful note. Passive mentoring is taking place and important lessons are being conveyed.

Intentional mentoring requires deliberate and thoughtful planning. Choosing a mentor and choosing a protégé is like investing. Successful mentors are vigilant and discerning of the traits, talents, and interests of their junior personnel and are careful to embark on mentorships with only those who match them well. Similarly, purposeful protégés will identify the particular lessons and skills they desire to attain from the more experienced mentor, and will seek to honor those shared values with an investment of a part of their own life of learning and modeling.

Intentional mentoring cannot take place with everyone in the musical ensemble, but formal and intentional mentoring can be accomplished with a special few. The primary difference is the degree of intensity, structure, and investment of time.

Are Mentors Born or Built?

Maturity has more to do with what types of experiences you've had, and what you've learned from them, and less to do with how many birthdays you've celebrated.

—author unknown

Any conductor who knows that mentoring takes place within the ensemble experience and knows that passive mentoring can lead to intentional mentoring with specific individuals must deal with the motivational realities of ensemble members and the protégé.

The successful conductor, the conductor to whom protégés look for a variety of lessons, will ask whether or not he or she can develop the traits the ensemble desires from its conductor.

Research shows that mentors that want to be mentors, typically are indeed good mentors. Apparently, the acknowledgment by an individual that he or she wants to pass on knowledge, skills, and life lessons to another individual is the leading indicator of the conductor and leader's eventual success in this process.

The observant and sensitive conductor-mentor will seek to enhance those opportunities and situations that advance the characteristics that make for a successful ensemble experience, and similarly, the observant and sensitive conductor-mentor will seek to eliminate those moments and situations that erode these characteristics.

To do so, the conductor-mentor begins the mentoring process by creating a mental dashboard that strategically monitors these positive and negative characteristics. All decisions pass by the monitoring dashboard, and all encounters with the ensemble, and individuals within the ensemble, pass by this dashboard. This dashboard, or group of filters, serves as a checklist for keeping the mentoring experience on track and positive.

Like the dashboard in any moving vehicle that monitors speed, fuel, engine temperature, wheel rotation, ground temperature, and mileage, the attentive conductor creates a mentoring dashboard for the environment that monitors enthusiasm, confidence, authority, honesty, transparency, encouragement, and friendship. These are the gauges that will serve to guide the successful mentoring relationship and that will be outlined in the chapters ahead.

Most conductors would not be in their current position without naturally possessing many of the traits that will become a part of the mentoring dashboard. However, to be systematic and intentional in the role of mentor, the gauges of the dashboard allow the conductor-mentor to remain vigilant and mindful in every encounter with the protégé, both when the lessons develop naturally and organically and when the lessons generate from another source of inspiration and pedagogy.

The mental dashboard will serve as both a checklist and a safeguard for the mentor as he or she develops a structure for an intentional mentoring relationship. The labeling of specific gauges is not casual, but comes from the results of research on the psychosocial dynamic of what protégés look for in a desired mentor.

Thought Experiment

Creating a dashboard icon that is most compelling to you, what shape does your dashboard and its various component gauges take? As a musician, could it take the shape of a metronome or recording mixing board? Could it take the shape of a motorized vehicle? Could it take the shape of gauges on a kitchen appliance?

- After constructing your own mental dashboard, which gauges do you consider vital and most significant as you remain vigilant to the professional requirements of your work and behavior?

- After naming those professional requirement elements, where would you place them on your mental dashboard?

- After establishing the vital gauges, which additional gauges do you consider important but secondary to the vital elements of the professional focus listed above?

- After naming those secondary areas, give them a visual place, but not the same place of prominence on your dashboard.

HEARING THE VOICE

Beginning the Mentoring Process and Relationship

In every art beginners must start with models of those who have practiced the same art before them. And it is not only a matter of looking at the drawings, paintings, musical compositions, and poems that have been and are being created; it is a matter of being drawn into the individual work of art, of realizing that it has been made by a real human being, and trying to discover the secret of its creation.

—Ruth Whitman

In business settings, research findings demonstrate that mentorships that begin informally are often more effective than those brokered or arranged by a third party. Informal beginnings are most likely the norm in the setting of the musical ensemble.

The keen ensemble director can make such determinations in response to informal inquiries and signals from a developing or emerging protégé, which can lead to intentional mentoring relationships.

The purpose of the following exercise is to give focus to the mentoring process. The exercise is one that I perform with a group to demonstrate the intentional aspect of what we do in the mentoring process. This exercise is not intended to teach you how to mentor, but rather, how mentoring works.

Thought Experiment

I begin my experiment by writing a sentence from Leo Tolstoy's short story, *Where Love is, God Is*, on a piece of paper:

> *In a certain town there lived a shoemaker who was called Martin.*

Then I ask the group to create and add a sentence to Tolstoy's opening line, then pass the growing story around the room, each person adding one sentence, then passing it on to the next person, each adding a new sentence to the developing narrative. I ask the group to simply make the story interesting and to make it better. The writing continues until everyone has added a sentence, passing the story on.

The result of this exercise, with the topic of mentoring in mind, is remarkable, and demonstrates the mentoring process. As the story grows, one person adds color or detail to the preceding sentence. Another takes the story in a new direction, while another will take that new direction and add depth. The exercise becomes a mentoring process of taking something that is good, and even classic, adding something creative and unique, and then passing it on, making the story better and better.

The written drama is creative and by the end of the short exercise, a delightful story results. As people take a good work in progress, add their creativity and then pass it on, mentoring takes place before their eyes. In the end, the story they created bears no resemblance to Tolstoy's original masterpiece, but it is nevertheless a good story.

In the artistic community, we call it "finding your voice." In the faith community, we call it "hearing a call." In the business community, we call it "discovering your strengths." But regardless of your center of work activity, the larger quest is every individual's pursuit of a place in the creative process.

Finding one's place in the creative process could not be more natural for human creatures, since any exploration of the generative cycle leads us back to creation. This journey to the creative source takes us to where each person fits in the generative flow—from parents, to teachers, to citizens, to colleagues, to workers, and/or volunteers.

And in this generative flow, the possible places in which we find ourselves creating are endless. For one it might be a cross-stitch design; for another, a relationship; for another, their first guitar; for another, a thoughtfully prepared meal; for another, a technical solution to a problem; for another, organizational contribution in the neighborhood; for another, religious reform; for another, the choice of clothing worn on a given day; for another, the design of a cathedral.

For others, the generative flow takes place by performing in an ensemble under the leadership of a capable conductor. The length of time can be weeks, months, or years, but anyone participating in an ensemble is part of it.

For any of us that have ever wanted to give back or give forward, the topic of generativity is not a casual issue. For conductors and teachers, part of our own "voice finding" or "call hearing" is very much involved in the topic of generativity, or mentoring.

As a conductor, the percentage of those ensemble members gathering to rehearse and perform each week, who wish to go beyond technical advancement by looking to the conductor for more than the shaping of a phrase, is a small but significant number. The fact that this number exists in the research as a percentage is compelling. The statistic of one member out of four in the ensemble choosing to be there because of the conductor is persuasive, and any responsible conductor must take it seriously.

Without a doubt, the majority of musicians in our ensembles are looking to the conductor for musical direction and instruction on how to shape a phrase. There are some, however, that are looking to the conductor to shape part of their vocation and life.

The Mentor as Leader

The signs of outstanding leadership appear primarily among the followers. Are the followers reaching their potential? Are they learning? Serving? Do they achieve the required results? Do they change with grace? Manage conflict?

—Max De Pree

A conductor by definition has stepped into a highly visible position of leadership. In recent years, energy and research has been devoted to the area of leadership development. Jim Collins identifies several characteristics that define a leader attempting to become increasingly more effective in his or her role.

As you read through this summary of Collins's leadership keys, it is instructive to reflect on the specific tasks a conductor is responsible for in the rehearsal and performance environment, as well as those tasks that lead to a sustainable and successful musical organization.

Furthermore, as you consider and start to build your mentoring mental dashboard, keep these leadership gauges in mind for possible inclusion to your guiding ideas and decision-making filters:

- Leaders channel their ego needs away from themselves and into a larger goal of building a great organization.

The goal of every conductor must always be to create a musical performance that represents a composer's intentions, brings inspiration to the performing musicians and audience, and contributes to the vitality and continuity of the artistic mission. The conductor's personality must disappear into the desired goal of a worthy performance so that the music can be truly heard and experienced. Within the boundary of a composer's intentions, performance practice, and refined musicianship, there is indeed room for interpretation on the part of the conductor—that is without question. But what defines a good leader is his or her ability to channel ego needs away from the higher purpose of the music. A strong image embodying the work of the conductor is of him or her facing the ensemble, conveying all that he or she knows and believes about the music, with back to the audience.

- Leaders first ask "Who?" and then "What?" by getting the right people doing the right job.

The conductor must build an ensemble of good musicians, and must choose quality and appropriate musical literature for the ensemble to perform its best. Both "who" and "what" are integrally related to best performance. "Who" for the conductor means sopranos, altos, tenors, basses, string players, wind players, brass players, and percussionists. "What" for the conductor means the musical score and the musical program. "Who" for the conductor-mentor may also lead to the identification of protégés, both passive and intentional.

- Leaders are brutally honest about the situation and current reality.

The conductor must first analyze and identify every potential problem, every weakness, and every flaw, which will determine the course of action to follow. Every detail must be analyzed and a proper course of action identified that will lead to correction, improvement, and finally worthy performance. This analysis takes place with the musical score, with the performing forces, and with every other factor that influences the rehearsal process and the performance. The protégé is the recipient of this analysis and of the passion, knowledge, and skill that lays the path on the journey from imperfection toward perfection.

For the conductor-mentor, such brutal honesty, though delivered with compassion and with the best interest of the protégé in mind, is one of the most important tasks of mentoring. Failing to offer constructive criticism to a protégé means partial failure for the mentorship. Avoiding constructive criticism can signal that the mentor is not interested in the process, and might even signal incompetence. While always affirming, appraisal is one of the primary areas a protégé seeks in a mentor.

- Leaders realize they are the best at what they do, and are doing what they are best at doing, working at what they are deeply passionate about doing, and doing what is best to move their organization forward.

It is easy to identify the conductor—he or she is the person in front, standing upright in full view of everyone, and clearly in charge. The conductor is there because he or she has the preparation and skills to lead, and is the best at conducting the ensemble. Certainly, there are other good conductors in the world. And certainly, conductors are replaceable. But for each leader-conductor, it is important to remember that the only one standing on the podium at this point in time is the person who is best at what he or she does.

- Leaders build the vision for the organization.

The conductor is the artistic director for the ensemble, charting a course for performances by the organization. The conductor develops a direction for the organization. While others are essential in the accomplishment of the work of the ensemble, the conductor builds the vision for the ensemble and lays out the plan for attaining the vision.

The conductor-mentor offers the "big picture" view to the protégé, helping the protégé look beyond his or her own challenges and personal hurdles. Mentors demonstrate how challenges can be building-block opportunities in a journey toward a bigger picture.

- Leaders create and affirm a core ideology and an envisioned future.

The conductor not only gives a faithful and inspired interpretation of the musical score, but also participates in sustaining the mission of the ensemble to assure that the performing organization remains relevant in concert seasons yet to come.

Built upon a solid core of musicianship and informed musical interpretation, the effective conductor demonstrates the traits of the exceptional leader, all within an ensemble environment that intensely pursues the shared task of musical accomplishment and the pursuit of excellence.

The Ongoing Process of Generativity

One thing I know; the only ones among you who will be really happy are those who will have sought and found how to serve.
—Albert Schweitzer

Erikson created the term "generativity" to denote "a concern for establishing and guiding the next generation." We express generativity in a variety of ways. I experience it as I raise my daughter. I experience it when I read my father's genealogical research as he traces our family history. I experience it when I visit with relatives at family gatherings over holidays. I experience it when I read an autobiography.

Generativity can be expressed in hundreds of ways, such as when we attend a community neighborhood meeting, create a support group, or in any other way a person tries to make a difference, either giving back, giving forward, or generally taking care of others.

In bluegrass musician Ralph Stanley's autobiography, he speaks of a defining moment that signaled the process of generativity is his life. At the age of eight, on one particular Sunday at the Point Truth Primitive Baptist Church in Scott County, Virginia, his dad put his hand on the young singer's shoulder and asked him to line out the hymn for the congregation to sing.

> On this Sunday morning, my family was sitting all bunched together on the pew-bench like usual: my dad, Lee, and my mother, Lucy, and my older brother, Carter, and me. There was a song my dad wanted to lead on. It was from the old Goble hymnbook: "Salvation, O! The Name I Love." It was one of his favorites, but he never could remember how the song started out. So he laid his hand on my shoulder and he called on me to start the song, to line it out for the congregation. (p. 3)

Stanley continues:

> So I took a deep breath and sung [sic] out the opening line the best I could. (p. 5)

For Stanley, this was the culmination of a mentoring process that had occurred by observation, week in and week out, until his mentor-father provided a moment of opportunity and affirmation.

As conductors, we experience generativity and the passive mentoring process every time we stand in front of our ensemble. Whether the purpose is pedagogical, related specifically to breathing or diction, or whether the purpose is to mentor in the areas of values and life balance, the process is ongoing and undeniable.

The foundation of this process of transformation is rooted in China's ancient classic, *I Ching*. *I Ching* has been studied with equal respect by generations of Taoists, Buddhists, and Confucians. Both traditional and contemporary Confucian scholars have pointed out that what the *I Ching* teaches is that the very nature of the Tao (The Way, the Path, the Course) is defined as *shengsheng buxi*, or generativity without ceasing. The reduplicative shengsheng means birth upon birth, or the constant generation of myriad things.

This is what humans do for each other, whether passively or intentionally. The process is universal. I draw attention to both this common and this ancient reference in order to expose the delusion of any thought of a "self-made" individual, as if there is a way to find one's individual voice without the assistance of other voices.

According to Berthrong, we learn two things from traditional Chinese teachings about creativity. First, creativity is the nature of the cosmos, now and forever. But simply *being creative* isn't enough. Human beings must find a way to be creative in a just and appropriate fashion, utilizing all the wisdom, discernment, and compassion at our disposal. Second, individual persons are not isolated or disconnected from other humans and the earth. We must test our creativity with a concern for the insight that we are parts of the vast web of creation and have a responsibility to heaven, earth, and humanity to assist in the flourishing of all creatures, great and small. The earth is our home, and we have a tremendous need for true creativity in becoming good neighbors for all our relations.

When we look beneath the creativity and genius of the great conductors, or when we observe the breakthroughs and innovations of industry leaders, we will inevitably discover the process of generativity in the axioms, lessons, experiments, and insights that the mentor passes on to the protégé.

The Mentoring Environment

Maturity consists of no longer being taken in by oneself.
—author unkown

The environment and community that we define as the musical ensemble is a unique setting for mentoring to take place. Therefore, it is imperative that the conductor-mentor understands the atmosphere the protégé needs and is looking for in the rehearsal setting and the mentoring process.

The following research conducted by Chuang at the University of Maryland provides insight into this unique psychosocial environment. This research highlights the traits necessary to be an effective mentor within the ensemble rehearsal environment. The desirable characteristics central to this research are in addition to musical assets such as musicianship, interpretive skills, performance ability, and other foundational musical characteristics expected of a conductor-leader.

In the process of conducting this research, ensemble members participated in a survey. Their response to the question, "What are the three most important characteristics that a conductor possesses?" resulted in the percentages shown below. These are the conductor characteristics that received the highest rankings of all characteristics surveyed. These characteristics also reflect the same traits that undoubtedly drew many of us to the leaders we observed and sought to emulate in our own professional life.

Enthusiasm	26%
Confidence	21%
Authority	17%

Stated in the narrative, ensemble members and the protégé are looking for a conductor that is passionate, demonstrates confidence as a leader, and is clearly knowledgeable about the subject. These three personality traits—enthusiasm, confidence, and authority—are the characteristics that should permeate the rehearsal environment in order to gain the respect of the ensemble members.

As seen earlier, the same traits—enthusiasm, confidence, and authority—characterize the excellent leader. These traits reflect a conductor's purpose and passion for his or her work, knowledge and skill base, and demonstrated sense of authority.

I spent a summer as a conducting student at the Aspen Music Festival, the renowned summer music institute in Aspen, Colorado. Every week we performed choral masterworks, all under the big Aspen tent, and all under the baton of different conductors. Each conductor had to quickly earn the respect of the performers and each had to accelerate the rehearsal process to keep pace with a demanding performance schedule. While techniques, personalities, and even languages varied from maestro to maestro, the common denominators among all the conductors were the sense of purpose, passion, confidence, and authority, which in turn, won the respect of the performers.

Conductors must accomplish success in score study, analysis, and comprehension and bind this with human understanding, skillful organization, time efficiency, and persuasiveness. Moreover, to be effective as a leader, the conductor must realize that the three characteristics of enthusiasm, confidence, and authority are the traits most appreciated by ensemble member and potential protégé. Of course, all of these successful musical disciplines contribute directly to a conductor's enthusiasm, confidence, and authority.

While personal charisma is generally impressive, for the long term, nothing will take the place of knowledge and refined skill. When asked if emotional self-control is an important trait for the conductor, 76 percent of ensemble members responded "yes," and another 15 percent responded "rather important." It is overwhelmingly clear that while the ensemble member is desirous of an enthusiastic leader, simultaneously, enthusiasm must be channeled through emotional self-control on the part of the conductor-mentor. Recalling Collins's characteristics of great leadership—Leaders channel their ego needs away from themselves and into a larger goal of building a great organization. (Jim Collins, p. 39)

Thought Experiment

Reflect on your own experience of leadership. Where do the essential traits of enthusiasm, confidence, and authority come from? Further, when you feel that you genuinely experience these traits through your mentors, how are these traits manifested?

To direct this reflection in the negative, describe encounters you have experienced in which false expressions of enthusiasm, confidence, and authority were on display. How did you know these expressions were insincere? What could the leader have done to dispel the perception of these false impressions?

The Ensemble Mentoring Environment

Maturity of mind is the capacity to endure uncertainty.
—John Finley

Although the thoroughly prepared, musically solid, enthusiastic, confident, and authoritative conductor-mentor ascends the podium with definite ideas for the rehearsal and ultimate performance of the music at hand, he or she might still make mistakes and might even change his or her opinion about various aspects of the music. This reality creates an environment of vulnerability for any leader, especially if the leader somehow believes that there can be no turning back from an earlier statement or position.

As careful and knowledgeable as a conductor is, ongoing study and exposure to new information can reveal mistakes, flaws in interpretation, faulty research, and a variety of other reasons that could cause a conductor to have a change of mind.

This issue for the conductor as mentor is not so much the difficulty of a simple change of mind, but rather how this change is handled in full view of the ensemble. Research makes it clear that ensemble members do not expect their conductor to be without flaw, nor to sustain or convey an image of perfection. In fact, research shows ensemble members prefer an environment of honesty and transparency from their conductor.

When Chuang's research asked, "How should a conductor react to their own mistakes?," over 75 percent of those responding said, "Admit them and try to improve," while the balance said, "Admit them and apologize." When ensemble members were asked if they thought a conductor would compromise professionalism if he or she acknowledged mistakes, 90 percent of responders answered "no."

Ensembles clearly prefer transparency and honesty from their leader, but with no disregard to authority and confidence in the subject matter. There have been times in my score study and rehearsal process that I have clung to first impressions and misreadings of a rhythm or pitch, and with best intentions even though mistaken, carried those mistakes into a rehearsal. When corrected in the actual rehearsal, I simply and humbly admit that I missed "that one," apologize for my error, correct the mistake, and then move on. The same thing happens from time to time in my conducting. When it does, I will point at myself on the occasion and immediate instance of those miscues, indicating an admission of error, and I try to learn from the mistake and never let it happen again at the same place. The humanness of personal correction has always created an increase in respect and confidence on the part of the ensemble, as opposed to the erosion of trust through an attempt at bluffing or covering up the error.

When ensemble members have been asked, "What kind of conductor do you most like working with?" their responses with regard to the following characteristics, came up in these percentages:

Encouraging	31%
Friendly	21%
Intense	20%
Relaxed	15%
Talkative	6%
Quiet	6%
Reserved	0%

Built upon a solid core of musicianship, the effective conductor-mentor establishes a foundation of enthusiasm, confidence, and authority, and works to further create an atmosphere of honesty, transparency, encouragement, and friendship, all within an ensemble environment that intensely pursues the shared task of musical accomplishment and perfection.

Of special note, the recurring theme of "encouragement" appears over and over in the literature related to mentor and protégé. The nod of affirmation and approval was identified earlier as the most powerful mentoring tool at work in the mentoring process.

It is interesting to note that ensemble members are almost evenly divided in their preference of a "relaxed" conductor over an "intense" conductor, and evenly opinioned regarding a "talkative" conductor and a "quiet" conductor. A reserved conductor is apparently an anomaly.

We can now return to the mentoring mental dashboard with a strong affirmation on the gauge that monitors an ensemble environment that is encouraging. The reaction by ensemble members makes it clear that this element is in highest demand by performing individuals and should have a definite place in the focus and work of the conductor-mentor.

It is also clear that the ensemble members desire a degree of intensity in the pursuit of the ensemble objectives. Therefore the gauge should monitor the balance between intensity of pursuit and encouragement and support. Stated in conceptual terms, this is an environmental balance between challenge and nurture.

Thought Experiment

Creating a gauge with "nurture" on one end and "challenge" on the extreme opposite end, reflect and describe the incremental steps along the path leading from nurture to challenge. Terms may vary from "laugh" to "hand holding" to "comfort" on one extreme, and on the other, "push," "confuse," "break down," and "fail."

The point of this thought experiment is to help you focus on the continuum that runs between nurture and challenge, and to develop awareness about how equilibrium can be established and maintained.

Why Mentor, Why Protégé ?

Successful people turn everyone who can help them into sometime mentors.

—John Crosby

Members of an ensemble view the conductor as a leader within the organization and as a person with unique skills and personal traits. Those skills are intrinsic to leadership, with musical knowledge being a highly refined subset of these skills.

As established earlier, the conductor-mentor can be in the ongoing process of mentoring passively, due to the quiet, alternating active–passive encounters that take place in the setting of the rehearsal and performance environment. The conductor contributes from a bank of knowledge and experience to the process of musical preparation. In this ongoing situation, the conductor displays the qualities actively desired by those participating in the ensemble, and he or she is only passively aware that any of the performers desires become a protégé.

In order for the mentoring relationship to move from passive to active, certain conditions must exist. The potential mentor must have the knowledge, experience, desired skills, and valued qualities that the willing protégé desires to acquire. The protégé signals, in some manner, that he or she wishes to learn more about those qualities or skills from this mentor. Then the potential mentor must be willing to enter into this formal relationship and accept the implied responsibility.

Therefore, in order to move from a passive to an active role as a mentor, signaled intentions must come from both the mentor and the protégé. Generally, the movement from a passive to an active mentoring relationship comes from the protégé; however, the motivation to enter into this active relationship can be prompted by any of three entities: the mentor, the protégé, and/or the sponsoring organization.

Whether or not the process in place to advance the activity of mentoring is formal, there should be no hindrance to the process of generativity. For the willing mentor, the spark can come from a question, the prolonged interest in a topic, or a heightened attentiveness to any aspect of the work.

Motivation is categorized as either extrinsic or intrinsic, with extrinsic rewards coming from the environment surrounding an individual and intrinsic rewards coming from within the individual.

Daniel Pink speaks of motivation in contemporary terms by classifying the evolution and types of motivation using software development terms—Motivation 1.0, Motivation 2.0, and Motivation 3.0.

In Pink's taxonomy, Motivation 1.0 is the primitive incentive for survival, while Motivation 2.0 consists of the "sticks and carrots" system of extrinsic rewards and punishments. Motivation 3.0 comes as a result of the desire for autonomy, mastery, and purpose. In 21st-century developed society, Motivation 3.0 is at work.

Nothing could more perfectly describe the process of generativity than Pink's modern model of autonomy, mastery, and purpose. These intrinsic rewards are the commonalities that unite mentor and protégé, and speak to the contemporary significance of the mentor-protégé dynamic.

Intrinsic benefits for the mentor include personal satisfaction and fulfillment; increased creativity and rejuvenation; reenergized working environment as a result of working with talented and energetic protégés; increased support from both the protégé base and the sponsoring organization; personal satisfaction from helping another grow in the process of generativity; and the opportunity to help shape the next generation within the profession.

For most conductor-mentors, intrinsic motivation is the prevailing driver at work in the mentor-protégé experience. However, extrinsic benefits can also be at work and available to the mentor in intentional and formal mentorships.

Extrinsic benefits for the mentor may include a reduction in workload, technical assistance, improved professional identity, greater professional competence, increased career satisfaction, decreased job stress, development of a loyal support base, professional recognition, financial rewards, and network enhancement.

The cost of mentorship comes first and foremost in the areas of time and energy invested in both the protégé and the process. Risks come in the form of failed expectations, disloyalty, dishonesty, jealousy, and moral failures. More will be said later about safeguards to put into place on the mentor's personal mental dashboard to guard against potential negative risks.

Potential rewards to motivate a protégé to move into an active, intentional, or formal mentorship include: greater professional competence, improved professional identity, enhanced promotion rates, higher salaries, accelerated career mobility, increased career satisfaction, greater acceptance within the organization, and decreased job stress and role conflict. Research shows that mentored individuals are also more likely to mentor others in the future.

Organizations that intentionally establish professional connections between mentor and protégé, may reap tangible benefits through increased productivity in the workplace, enhanced organizational commitment from both mentor and protégé, decreased employee turnover, and accelerated development of talent within the organization.

Having outlined the intrinsic and extrinsic benefits of mentoring, the primary driving motivation for the mentoring process remains the desire for generativity in vocation and life, and the desire of the individual mentor to give back, and to give forward. Mentoring is shallow if not motivated by the care and concern on the part of the mentor for the passing on of values and best practices to an interested and eager protégé.

RESPONDING TO THE VOICE

Moving to Mentoring

Leadership should be born out of the understanding of the needs of those who would be affected by it.

—Marian Anderson

As conductor-leader-mentor, the ensemble leader may work with as few as a dozen individuals or as many as a hundred. Further, the conductor may work with one ensemble, or may conduct several performing groups. No matter the number of performers or the number of ensembles, research tells us that three out of four performers in the ensemble are there for the music. And most healthy conductors would remark, "and that is the way it should be."

But what about those other individuals in Chuang's three-out-of-four statistic: why are they there? Twenty-five percent of ensemble members state that the conductor, in addition to the music and the experience, is the significant reason for their continuing participation in the ensemble. Could it be that potential protégés exist within this particular statistic?

To be sure, there are clearly other important reasons why a person chooses to perform in an ensemble. Those reasons might include wanting to take the opportunity to work and learn from other musicians and to experience making music in an ensemble; having an interest in the literature rehearsed and performed and in the community formed by the individuals making up the ensemble; and a desire to develop personal musical skills, as well as other important and healthy factors. In a very real sense, the musical community of the ensemble also serves as a mentor to the individual.

However, it is equally clear that each of these areas of musical growth also relates to the personal mentoring process, since it is the conductor that influences the makeup of the overall musical community, the literature chosen for rehearsal and performance, and the core issues related to personal leadership. The mentoring conductor is mindful that the process of generativity permeates these choices.

Focusing on the one-in-four performers listing the conductor as the primary reason they remain with the ensemble, it is apparent these performers are present due to their desire to learn from the conductor.[1]

1 Chuang's research assumes that there are ensembles where financial decisions override a choice in the matter, such as a professional ensemble, a scholarship, or other incentives. Further, there are situations where performers have no choice, and if they want to perform, they perform under the leadership provided.

Outside the intentional process of an institution or other organization designating and assigning a mentor to a protégé, or assigning a protégé to a mentor, the natural question must be, "How does the mentor-protégé relationship move from informal to formal?"

The essential catalyst for this process to take place is that the mentor must show an intentional pedagogical interest in the protégé, or the protégé must signal an intentional desire to learn from the conductor.

The study by Levine and Crom on the psychology of the success of Dale Carnegie revealed the basic fact that individuals are flattered when others pay attention to them. For the potential protégé, the first indication that there could be a mentor-protégé relationship is when the future mentor shows an interest in the professional development of the protégé. Similarly, the mentor understands that by the protégé's expression of professional interest to the mentor-conductor, that this ensemble member wants to learn more than what is available in the basic conductor–ensemble relationship.

We want to be around people who show an interest in us. We tend to reciprocate their interest by showing interest in them. This interest must be genuine and intrinsic for the mentor because the investment of precious resources of time and energy will not be casual in the intentional mentoring process. The mentor must see something in the protégé that motivates the mentor to care. The protégé must project his or her need to learn something unique from the mentor.

This exploration leads us to the personal characteristics a protégé seeks in a mentor. The protégé seeks lessons that go beyond demonstrated technical skills and perfected theories, and that speak to the perceived relationship between protégé and mentor. These characteristics relate directly to the protégé's reason for staying in an ensemble.

Research indicates that the ideal mentor demonstrates the following characteristics of professional interest to the protégé:

EXUDES WARMTH

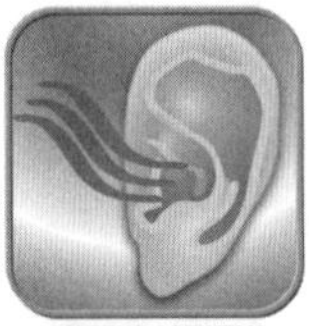
LISTENS ACTIVELY

USES POWER CONSTRUCTIVELY

EXUDES EXCITEMENT AND POSSIBILITY

- Exudes warmth
- Listens actively
- Uses power constructively
- Exudes excitement and possibility
- Is actively engaged in their profession
- Demonstrates balance of profession and lifestyle
- Demonstrates networks of collaboration
- Shares the network of their discipline and colleagues
- Shows unconditional regard
- Tolerates idealization with grace
- Embraces humor
- Expects excellence in effort, not perfection
- Attends to interpersonal cues
- Is trustworthy

- Respects values
- Does not stoop to jealousy
- Is humble, modest, and conservative
- Is nonmaleficent (will do no harm)

Returning to the earlier image of the dashboard, the items on the list above represent the gauges and the foci for vigilant monitoring that must be a part of the mentor's mental dashboard.

In terms of formal aspects of a vocation, the mentor is actively involved in his or her profession. The mentor is a "frequent flyer" in terms of vocational activity and experience. As such, the mentor demonstrates a tangible model of how to be involved with and carry out the tasks and assignments within the profession. Further, the mentor does this while balancing a personal life in full view of the protégé.

On the other hand, for performers participating in vocational pursuits outside the musical arts, the ensemble as metaphor and the conductor as mentor, have applications to many professions. It is not unusual for a non-musician to want to participate in a mentoring relationship with an ensemble conductor.

In terms of interpersonal communication, the mentor has characteristics that are valuable to the protégé in helping shape skills toward future leadership; these characteristics are essential in creating a teaching environment that maintains the balance between nurture and challenge.

Thought Experiment

Reflecting on the creation of gauges for the mentor's emerging mental dashboard, study the list of mentor characteristics listed in the table above. Consider how to construct a mentor-protégé environment and relationship that carefully monitors attention to these important traits.

- What habits and behaviors augment the needs of the protégé?
- What habits and behaviors distract from the needs of the protégé?
- What personal traits and characteristics are absent from this ideal list?

The Imperative of Interconnectedness

To do right is wonderful. To teach others to do right is even more wonderful.

—Mark Twain

In a recent interview, former U.S. president Bill Clinton spoke to the idea of our connectedness to each other as he defined his approach to any profound issue that he faces:

> My simple premise is that the mission of the 21st century is to build up the positive and reduce the negative forces of interdependence…I'll ask myself on any profound issue: will this increase positive interdependence or reduce negative interdependence? (*Newsweek*, December 28, 2009)

Connecting this interdependence with the goal of intentional generativity is not an easy process. Returning to my genesis question, "Who openly declares to another they either are willing to mentor, or are seeking a mentor?" Establishing this connection is a challenging first step for mentor and protégé.

In Malcolm Gladwell's book *What the Dog Saw*, the author offers insight into the difficulty inherent in such a generative process. Gladwell says, "Our instinct as humans, after all, is to assume that most things are not interesting." (p. xiii) I extend that statement to not only things, but also to those individuals we encounter that could potentially serve as mentors.

Part of the process of generativity is for a protégé to be interested in what otherwise might be uninteresting and to look for mentors that might not look interesting or heroic at first glance. The same pursuit of potential interest is true as mentors look to discover potential in protégés.

In truth, what further complicates this process and pursuit is that we might expect a mentor to be able to articulate his or her greatness, and to be able to communicate to the protégé the secrets of his or her own success. Andrew Carnegie is credited with saying, "As I grow older, I pay less attention to what men [sic] say. I just watch what they do." I agree with Carnegie. Who, really, will tell you the secret of their success? And why would they? And why should they? Persons of greatness are unlikely to have analyzed the nuances of their own greatness and if they have, would it be wise for them to articulate it publicly?

It has been my experience that important and significant lessons are more readily "caught" than "taught," and once again, this is where the mentoring process gains credibility. By observing each other, and by staying in proximity to each other, lessons can be discovered, tested, and evaluated. In the best of mentoring environments, this is the essential flow.

My life of learning has revolved around the people and theories of the academy and the life lessons of mentors in that environment. Sometimes theory and mentorship came together at the same place. At other times, I found one through the other. Over the last two decades, I sought mentors in areas and in vocational arenas where I wanted to grow personally, and I have sought out such people purposefully outside the protective walls of the academy.

In my experience as protégé, I am indebted to mentors that worked vocationally as carpenters, sound engineers, college presidents, small business owners, preschool teachers, college faculty colleagues, a variety of entrepreneurs, and other musical conductors. In my experience as mentor, I have enjoyed the opportunity to influence a variety of protégés with backgrounds as diverse as my mentors. I do not intend to stop either role or relationship.

Gladwell gives additional insight into this mentoring pursuit as he distinguishes between the "powerful" and the "knowledgeable." As a writer, when he is looking for an interesting story, he says that starting at the top may prove finding the story difficult. However, he has observed that people in the middle may be willing to share: "People at the top are self-conscious about what they say (and rightfully so) because they have position and privilege to protect—and self-consciousness is the enemy of 'interestingness.'" (p. xiv) This is less likely to be the case for those in the middle. And the fact is, most of the world is "in the middle."

A few years ago, I noticed my answer to a rather frequently asked question began taking new shape. As I attended conferences and networked with students and conductors—

many wanting to return to school for more formal education—I was often asked, "where do you recommend I study?" As I listened carefully in order to discern their need, I became aware of the difference between educational credentials—with the inherent and important canon of ideas, theories, and skills—in contrast to a somewhat different motivation, which we develop as we mature, for personal growth, vocational definition, and new mental challenges. In my response to their question, I found it necessary to differentiate between these two separate areas of study—formal study and credentialing, and informal observation and mentoring.

In terms of credentialing and acquiring skills, exploring the canon of ideas that shape civilization, and learning in an environment of others seeking similar intellectual pursuits, the quest becomes a matter of putting in the time and doing the homework to find the academies that have the structures and proven programs that match a person's most intense vocational pursuits and calling. There is no doubt that one's preparation should include methodically studying the repertoire of approaches to life's questions and dilemmas. That preparation involves hard work exemplified by approaches from contrasting and developing critical thinking skills on complex issues, to learning how to play a C major scale on piano.

In terms of observing and learning the values and skills of a proven master or professional, and learning in the context of a real-world and functioning environment, the protégé will identify a mentor that has traveled the road before, and the protégé will seek to learn from the acquired knowledge, lessons, and experiences of that willing mentor. The richness of the human experience is playing out all around the protégé seeking a guide in his or her pursuits. Those pursuits will include lessons gained from specific technical choices, to the very essence of a life calling.

Our interconnectedness, for individuals and professionals, as well as for the mentor who inherently desires to contribute positively to the process of generativity, is good news for the mentoring process, and is good news for the protégé in the ensemble setting. The mentor-protégé relationship within the ensemble arts is not dependant upon matriculation, registration, tuition, or any of the well-defined and structured processes of formal education (although these still may be present); it is, however, dependant upon an agreement between mentor and protégé to trust each other in a defined mentoring process.

Skill Set

Do all the good you can, By all the means you can, In all the ways you can, In all the places you can, To all the people you can, As long as ever you can.

—John Wesley

There was a point in my hobby time of banjo playing when I approached a faculty colleague in the school of music, Raymond McClain, for some coaching toward my personal banjo "picking." I was the choral director at the school and Raymond, a member of the legendary McClain Family Band from Berea, Kentucky, was the faculty coach of the resident bluegrass ensemble and teacher of mandolin and banjo.

I told Raymond I was bored with my banjo playing and needed a new picking pattern. He listened to my complaint, quickly considered my request, and casually sketched out a new picking pattern in tablature on a napkin. The new suggested "roll" that he outlined was not particularly unique, but underneath it he wrote, "x 10,000" (multiplied 10,000 times). The real lesson, as well as the reality, was that the picking pattern was simple but the time needed to master the pattern was a serious investment of time and effort—repeated 10,000 times.

In terms of acquiring skills and becoming proficient or possibly expert at those skills, the current wisdom asserts that expertise comes as a result of 10,000 hours of purposeful, directed time focused on the desired discipline or skill. Current research has qualified this number as the necessary benchmark for creating mastery of any specific skill area. (The coincidence that the coaching McClain gave me to practice the banjo picking pattern "x 10,000" and the standard of 10,000 practice hours for mastery, is truly a numerical coincidence. However, that coincidence certainly got my attention.)

However, beyond credentials and skill mastery, there remains the "where do I go?" question throughout life as generativity continues, and as individuals seek guidance for those hours of invested time. The "then what?" that follows the academy and formal training, as well as the lifelong pursuit of "why," involves the relationship and assistance of a mentor.

My response to those asking about the ongoing process of generativity has been more and more about identifying a mentor or mentors. The ensemble experience, a silent and ancient environment, presents this reality to many that would seek to be a protégé to a conductor-mentor.

It is the fortunate protégé that realizes the world is vibrant with mentoring potential, readily available for the one that recognizes that there is still something to learn and plenty of people from whom to learn.

The mentor is the person able to demonstrate the solid foundation upon which the protégé truly wants to build their own vocation and life balance. The mentor knows the axioms of the trade. This is a person that can teach principles and values.

The mentor may or may not have already mastered technique or theory, but is still working at it. A mentor is able to excite the wonder and inspiration for a particular area, even after years and years of practice. The mentor has the confidence that comes by means of repeated successes, but has not yet reached satisfaction with his or her own success.

I recall an early mentor who observed my fascination with the rehearsal and performance of my first G. F. Handel oratorio in his choir. I was impressed by the ease and comfort by which my mentor approached the score, and I was amazed by the power of the music. My mentor was taken by my enthusiasm for this masterpiece, and not long into this relationship, he gave me access to his office so that I could listen to my choice of the hundreds of recordings and musical scores in his collection. Throughout my mentor-protégé relationship with this conductor, he would ask me what I had recently found interesting or had listened to in his library. We discussed many works that he had never performed, or would ever perform.

Thought Experiment

- Reflecting forward, think of individuals in your immediate circle of activity that have demonstrated the traits of a mentor.

- Reflecting forward, think of individuals in your immediate circle of activity that have demonstrated the traits of a protégé.

The Protégé and the Mentor

What lies behind us and what lies before us are tiny matters compared to what lies within us.

—Oliver Wendell Holmes

As a protégé, I didn't expect my mentors to tell me the secrets of their success. I only appreciated their willingness to give me proximity to them and to observe their process of work so I could discover those axioms and secrets on my own. In fact, I have to even wonder if I would have been quite so teachable and open to my mentors if I knew they could even articulate their refined abilities. Research demonstrates that the most effective mentors are indeed humble when it comes to demonstrating their abilities. While it might have been exciting for me to recognize that my mentors were that self-aware, I suspect I would also be slightly skeptical if I realized they knew and controlled their own magic wand.

The traits in the list below represent the foundational elements I observed in my personal mentors. It comes from my personal reflection as a protégé to the mentors throughout my career. Whether or not I could articulate at the time what I was looking for, upon reflection, these are the traits I observed and acquired through those I list today as mentor. As I peruse my journals over the years, these categories come into focus as a result of my observations and writing:

- Career and life balance
- Intellectual curiosity
- Intellectual diplomacy and humility
- Spiritual integrity
- Interdependence
- Sense of true greatness

This list, while universal in application, still remains a personal list, based upon traits that mattered to me both vocationally and personally.

The following characteristics represent a broader set of traits for the ideal mentor. These key characteristics are the result of the research and writing on the mentor-protégé relationship:

A mentor gets a glimpse of the protégé's potential and sets good expectations.
A mentor realizes the protégé will be discouraged along the way.
A mentor has an eye out for the protégé.
A mentor will give the protégé "benefit of the doubt."
A mentor seeks to discover the best of what the protégé can do.
A mentor can step aside and give the protégé a chance.
A mentor is encouraging.

A mentor gives a protégé time and attention.
A mentor will be honest with the protégé about his or her strengths and weaknesses and offer words of encouragement and correction.
A mentor will not abuse a protégé.

Similarly, based upon the research and writing regarding the role of the protégé, the next list represents the desirable traits a mentor looks for in a protégé:

The protégé demonstrates to the mentor a sense of commitment, sacrifice, discipline, and exemplary work ethic.
The protégé comes to the mentor with goals and shows a personal spark toward those goals.
The protégé is willing to pay dues with the fundamentals of the trade.
The protégé is willing to follow the rules, which include the rules of personal responsibility, respect for authority, and desire for accountability.
The protégé has the right attitude, which begins with on-time arrival and proceeds with a delight in doing the work.
The protégé is teachable and willing and desiring to learn.
The protégé is trustworthy, both as a person and with the lessons taught.
The protégé is "worth the mentor's while," in the sense that the lessons gained will add to the process of ongoing generativity for the vocation, which constitutes the primary motivation for the mentor in doing this work.

As I enjoyed proximity to my mentors in order to learn the lessons I sought to learn from them, I listened to them as they struggled to articulate the inner workings that made them tick. Furthermore, I observed them carefully in their preparation, teaching, and practice. What made me their true protégé was not only the helpful things they said, but also their struggle, what they cared to talk about, how they tackled a problem, how they recovered from challenges and possible failures, what they devoted themselves to, and how they acted upon their convictions.

Thought Experiment

- As you reflect on the larger issues that you became aware of through the work and activity of a mentor, what traits have remained with you that could be categorized as your own set of foundational elements for the mentoring experience?
- For each foundational element listed, what implications do these categories or traits have for your own thinking toward mentor and protégé?

What We Learn and What We Do

Mentoring is a brain to pick, an ear to listen, and a push in the right direction.

—John C. Crosby

Research is clear on the subject of what protégés want from mentors: they want examples that can serve as models of how to balancc their professional and personal lives. To paraphrase Johnson and Ridley, a protégé wants to observe a congruent individual who has not only achieved some degree of success within his or her field, but also has demonstrated success in balancing life with profession.

Mindful mentors are self-aware; they see themselves as consistent with who they really are. They are not incongruent in that there is no gulf between the front (or veneer) they present to protégés and their internal sense of self-experience. The best mentor can just as easily pass on a lesson learned from experience, as say, "I don't know" when this is truly the case. There should be no shame or discomfort in such a situation, and any attempt to feign knowledge would be out of step for the congruent mentor.

According to Johnson and Ridley (pp. 87–88), the following congruencies exist within the life of a worthy mentor:

- **Theory and Practice** The protégé wants to see the mentor in action—not just espousing theories. The protégé wants to know how to set boundaries that balance work and non-work activity. In the back of the mind of every protégé is the nagging question, "Can I have a successful career and still have a satisfying personal life?" The protégé looks at the lifestyle of the mentor for an answer to this question.

- **Productivity** The best mentors are active, engaged participants in their chosen vocation. Effective mentors are fully engaged when it comes to their own professional landscape. They are deeply involved in the work of their discipline and are frequently in contact with colleagues and collaborators within the field. The protégé senses they cannot fully learn from another individual that has not traveled the desired road the protégé is also taking.

- **Authority in Action** When a mentor refuses to accept power and use authority constructively, the power of their position is inadvertently diminished. And while negative lessons are often as powerful as positive lessons, a protégé does not intentionally work with a mentor that only demonstrates negative lessons. Confidence and authority matter to the protégé when the mentor engages those traits.

- **Do No Harm** Abuse occurs when mentors fail to use their power to help protégés, especially when they are in the position or have the ability to do so. The failure to use power constructively can be as abusive as direct coercion.

- **Practice Humility** One interesting thread of mentoring research shows that mentors who underestimate the effectiveness of their leadership receive the highest quality-of-mentoring ratings from protégés. This trait of the good mentor suggests the importance of the power of humility toward influencing the protégé.

Thought Experiment

As musicians and conductors, we rely upon musical notation, interpretive symbols and our own unique score markings to guide us through a rehearsal. Reflect on the areas of congruency in the life of the mentor as outlined in this chapter, and imagine a symbol or graphic image for the sort of gauge that would represent each one of these areas if placed upon a mental dashboard. What image could represent the following guiding areas related to the mentor's influence on the protégé?

- Theory and Practice
- Productivity
- Authority in Action
- Do No Harm
- Practice Humility

The Primary Ethical Obligation of Mentors

People seldom improve when they have no other model but themselves to copy.

—Oliver Goldsmith

In their book *The Elements of Mentoring*, Johnson and Ridley explore the most fundamental ethical obligation mentors have to the protégé: *nonmaleficense* or "do no harm." This is the same motto of paramedics who are charged with the responsibility of transporting an accident victim or emergency patient to the hospital. At the very least, they are to do no harm in taking the patient from where they are, to where they need to be.

Johnson and Ridley outline four guidelines toward "doing no harm" while working with the protégé. These guidelines should be important warning gauges on the mental dashboard of every mentor:

- The mentorship must benefit the protégé.
- The mentorship prioritizes the professional and developmental needs of the protégé.
- Mentors treat protégés with dignity, respect, and compassion, even when protégés disappoint them.

- Mentors stay committed to the protégé, but accountable to the organization or the vocation.

In order to stay accountable to these four important guidelines, it is imperative to establish both a plan of action for the mentor-protégé experience and possibly third-party accountability for the process. Third-party accountability will help keep the relationship professional and in the event there is a problem, third-party accountability can help by becoming the termination agent that prevents any negative escalation of a problem.

Part of the plan of action should involve a journal of the process, which should include the careful documentation of observations, lessons, and activities. If both mentor and protégé keep such a professional log of activity, they can share this documentation with the third-party from time to time to establish transparent and honorable documentation of the experience.

This journal can be informal, as in a diary or chronicle of notes and ideas, or a structured outline of schedule, lessons, and tasks. For the mentor, the journal can construct the developing mental dashboard of gauges and guidelines, along with ideas and reflections related to the work of the protégé.

For the protégé, the journal will be full of observations, lessons, experiences, and reflections on lessons, and new lessons learned. No thought or idea is too insignificant for the reflections that become a part of this professional journaling process. Of all the books that come and go in the life of the mentor and protégé, the journals that result from the mentoring process will remain treasured volumes. I have several of them on my shelf, and I consult them as regularly as any other book in my library.

The act of journaling is a time-honored activity and discipline, and is a natural part of any intentional learning activity. If indeed many lessons are "caught" as readily and as easily as they are "taught," the journal that results from the mentoring experience becomes the receptacle for such learning. In good and healthy experiences, the journal becomes the reflective "textbook" of this professional experience. In circumstances when a problem arises, the journal would become documentation toward potential problem solving. In either situation, the journaling of the experience should begin at the outset of the mentor-protégé relationship and it should be shared periodically with a third party previously established. The third-party participant can add a very valuable and objective perspective on the experience.

Eby and colleagues investigated the conditions under which protégés are most likely to report negative mentoring experiences like abuse, neglect, intentional exclusion, tyranny, deception, incompetence, or sexual harassment. According to their research, with regard to the reporting of negative mentoring experiences, there is no correlation to a mentor who is one's supervisor or to the mentor who is not one's supervisor.

Excellent mentors will work to diffuse any problems that arise in the mentor-protégé relationship and will work actively to correct any misunderstandings. Involving a trusted colleague or third-party participant from the outset of the relationship establishes accountability and a healthy foundation for everyone—mentor, protégé, and institution or organization. Further, the ongoing discipline of keeping a journal helps establish a pattern of lessons, activities, and the all-important insights resulting from the experience.

Guidelines as the Mentor Begins

A true measure of your worth includes all the benefits others have gained from your success.

—Cullen Hightower

The mentor beginning to work in an intentional professional process with a protégé, needs to recognize the initial stages (shown below) of establishing the conditions in which the mentor-protégé relationship can grow. The mentor should carefully analyze these areas and consider them from the outset of the mentorship. Ongoing reflection will continue to help the mentor refine the mental dashboard that will guide the mentorship.

Know Your Protégé

There are three ways a mentor can positively challenge the protégé:

- Set expectations that are high enough to provide growth opportunities for the protégé.
- Set expectations that are challenging but not impossible for the protégé to accomplish.
- While insisting on excellence, also contribute confidence and affirmation to the protégé.

Affirm Your Protégé

The mentor should seek every opportunity to speak a kind and objective word, and to encourage, affirm, and keep the protégé on course. Further, the mentor should be prepared to be a sounding board for the protégé when needed.

The mentor should offer affirmation in the two areas the protégé has come to the mentor for life-lessons:

- Affirm the protégé as a professional.
- Affirm the protégé as a person.

Inform Your Protégé

- Mentors offer information and paths to knowledge for the protégé. This information and these paths are both professional and life affirming.
- When a mentor is friendly, open, approachable, and consistently encouraging, protégés are more at ease with risk-taking, more assured that they can succeed, and more comfortable asking for advice and assistance.

Be only a Mentor to Your Protégé

- Mentors do not gossip with the protégé.
- Mentors do not confuse friendship with mentoring.

It is very human for individuals (both mentor and protégé) to occasionally reflect on whether or not they are capable of truly doing what they are doing, and whether or not they are good at it. Perfection is an illusive goal, and sustaining that perfection, as worthy a pursuit as it is, is an ideal, not a reality.

Perfection and excellence are worthy goals, but lurking in the shadows of most healthy individuals is the thought they have not yet arrived at perfection. This feeling of "not yet arrived" has its negative manifestation in the "imposter syndrome," a condition that haunts individuals with the thought they are really not who they are trying to be.

The "imposter syndrome" haunts many a protégé, and without care, can be further amplified by the mentor. To help build a healthy confidence in the protégé, the sensitive mentor will be mindful of this possibility, and will work at developing the following personal traits that are essential for the protégé to reap the full benefit of the mentor-protégé process:

Exude warmth
Listen actively
Show unconditional regard
Tolerate idealization with grace and humility
Embrace humor
Do not expect perfection —expect excellence in effort
Attend to interpersonal cues
Be trustworthy
Respect values
Do not stoop to jealousy

Regarding the possibility of friendship developing out of the mentor-protégé relationship, investigations into whether mentoring relationships are "special" compared to regular supervisor–subordinate relationships found there are no significant differences between mentored subordinates and other subordinates, except those mentored reported higher levels of psychosocial functions such as friendship.

The significance of a mentor tolerating idealization with grace and humility will come into play if indeed a friendship results from the mentoring environment. Once again, placing this gauge on the mental dashboard helps the mentor to monitor a healthy relationship.

REFINING THE VOICE

Lessons from Greatness

We exist temporarily through what we take, but we live forever through what we give.

—Douglas M. Lawson

According to Jim Collins, one of the leadership factors leading to organizational greatness is that leaders channel their ego needs away from themselves and into a larger goal of building a great organization. (p. 39) Mentors live in the awareness that they are giving forward in life, not taking for themselves.

The reasons there are no more mentors than there are can be attributed to personal insecurity, individual ego needs, contemporary concept of success, focus on the end rather than the process, and lack of training or serious reflection in the process of mentoring.

Furthermore, success does not necessarily follow knowledge. A trained individual needs more help to apply the lessons they have learned. A mindful mentor will attend to the protégé's needs for additional supportive lessons to move their career along the path to success.

The following lessons must be a part of the experience a mentor creates for the protégé. The mentor must intentionally plan these lessons and integrate them into the observations, lessons, and coaching provided to the protégé:

Establish sense of self-worth and affirmation in the protégé's way of thinking.
Encourage and appropriately affirm the protégé's skills and talent.
Motivate the protégé toward solving ongoing curiosity.
Explore and embrace the "why?" of the vocation, current work, and life pursuits of the protégé.

For the protégé, the challenge is to observe the mentor on a regular basis. In order to adequately and meaningfully observe a mentor, the mentor must provide a certain amount of proximity to the protégé. The musical ensemble offers just the right routine proximity for observation.

When I coach life-long learners as they prepare for their vocation and other life skills, I encourage them to seek out successful individuals, and even greatness, and then to pay attention and take notes about their observations. If such proximity offers the chance to be a part of the action or to become active in an important pursuit, such as is the case when one participates in a musical ensemble, seize the opportunity, do well, and be keen to any instruction and insight that may come from the experience.

In my own pursuit of proximity, I have attempted to get into the environment of greatness. Gaining proximity to the action is the first and foremost step, whether at a school known for their great faculty and programs (great people are behind great programs), in great performing ensembles, in great functioning organizations, for admirable causes, or with a person of great results.

During my last sabbatical experience, I intentionally auditioned to sing in three unique choral ensembles, under three unique conductors, in order to mentor both informally and intentionally. As a protégé, my learning exploded into many directions, but proximity was a critical aspect of the mentoring environment.

Thought Experiment

Considering what is necessary for locating a mentoring environment or opportunity, reflect on the following pursuits:

- Locate "greatness" or "interestingness" in a person, program, organization, or cause.
- Determine how the environment affords personal proximity.
- Do not wait to be asked—discover how you can be of service and add value.
- Think of others that are pursuing what you are pursuing.
- Remember the proverb: "As iron sharpens iron, so one person sharpens another." (Proverbs 27:17)
- Keep the attitude positive—never give up.
- Remain the humble protégé, even if you become great yourself.

Locate Greatness

> *When you were born, you cried and the world rejoiced. Live your life so that when you die, the world cries and you rejoice.*
> —Cherokee proverb

As stated earlier, Malcolm Gladwell says, "Our instinct as humans...is to assume that most things are not interesting." In *What the Dog Saw*, Gladwell challenges this assumption with stories of great interest that come from ordinary individuals.

In the world of 21st century media, as reality shows dominate television ratings, one interesting development is that mundane and ordinary human behavior is of great interest to a great number of people. Many of the greatest reality show sensations over the last few years have been about the lives and talents of ordinary people.

Part of finding a mentor is to be interested in what otherwise may be uninteresting to other people, or even uninteresting to the mentor. Similar to finding a treasure in an antique shop, much of the treasure is in the eye and desire of the beholder, or in this study, the protégé.

It is important for the protégé to be able to verbalize and define what it is that he or she seeks to gain from a mentor. Are the keys to the successful mentor within their grasp of technical musical knowledge? Is the essence of the success of the desired mentor their ability to communicate to the ensemble? Is the ability to inspire at the heart of an effective mentor? Whatever the attributes or character, the protégé should be able to effectively name the trait or traits he or she seeks to acquire.

Defining what it is that the protégé wants to learn from the mentor is a critical step in in establishing goals and expectations. Does the protégé desire: Strategic expertise? Technical expertise? Professional awareness? Cultural awareness? Narrowing the list will help focus the mentorship.

What has a potential mentor accomplished that deserves modeling? Admiration for another person is normal, particularly if ongoing encounters have been very positive. A charismatic individual that draws people to them is a gifted person, but the would-be protégé should ask a fundamental question: "What is it that I am seeking to develop in my understanding of a discipline and set of skills?" Further, "What is the strength, the quality, I am attracted to?"

The setting of the musical ensemble brings into routine focus various leadership traits, as well as musical, technical, communication, inspiration, motivational, and a long list of other traits. Ensemble members observe and follow the directions of the conductor on a regular basis and have the opportunity to inspect any number of traits that are on public display.

Similarly, the aware conductor observes not only the ensemble as a whole, but also each of the individuals contributing to the musical ensemble. Over time, the keen conductor is able to naturally perform an analysis of most ensemble members in terms of strengths and weaknesses, not only musically, but also in other areas of personal behavior and performance. Qualifying whether or not a person is a "worthy" protégé should be a natural outgrowth of exposure over time through the ensemble experience.

To be thorough, when considering a mentor the protégé should also ask, "What am I not interested in?" Such a pursuit can and should result in a preferred list of desired abilities, systems, or styles. More often than not, the traits the protégé seeks in a mentor will be found in the nuances of practice, not in theory. Theories can be viewed objectively, while the leader's success in executing and accomplishing theories in the work context will play out in his or her actions and performance over time.

Other observations for the protégé to note would include whether or not others are interested in this person and if so, why? The reasons may range from specific knowledge to persuasive powers, rugged doggedness, and the knack for being at the right place at the right time. (How does one learn that?) Has this person produced other protégés in the past and if so, what do these protégés say about the experience working with the mentor?

The protégé should also consider, "Is the person consistent, or was that moment of brilliance a fluke?" This is not meant to discount anyone's significance, but we know that opportunities sometimes come to individuals at just the right time of need, that is, when they are "in the right place at the right time." We have also heard of the notion of the "Peter Principle," a humorous concept that rings true to some degree. The Peter Principle states, "In a hierarchy, every employee tends to rise to their level of *incompetence*." Being at the right place at the right time does not discount a person's need to have the right skills at those times and places. However, the skill level does need to be taken into account when considering a mentor. Another way to look at this question is, "Is the quality desired reproducible?" Be real about your expectations for the relationship.

Stop now and reflect—if your list is short, rethink these considerations before you go any further toward approaching the potential mentor. Ask the following questions:

- Have other protégés come from this mentor? If so, what have they said?
- Will I indeed enjoy proximity and learning time with this person?
- What steps do I think I need to take to reproduce the qualities I seek?
- Are such steps feasible?

If you think you are on the right track as you identify a potential mentor, then move forward and do not wait to be asked by the mentor. Approach the mentor and talk about your goals and personal expectations. If the mentor agrees to work with you, then consider moving forward with these efforts in establishing the desired mentorship environment.

- Build trust—trust is built one deed, one encounter, and one day at a time.
- If you make mistakes, own them and fix them. This is part of trust building and being "teachable."
- Be transparent—don't keep your life in a closet. The mentor is never sure what they are getting in a protégé, but if they are going to give honest glimpses of themselves, they must be able to trust you with what they share.

According to Elizabeth Collins, "Formal mentoring programs are, at best, a mixed success." She continues, "And even informal mentoring relationships often suffer shipwreck, with one or both parties disillusioned and frustrated." (Elizabeth Collins, p. 3) With this research-based warning in mind, the steps outlined earlier should be taken to construct a mentoring program and environment built on trust that results in a successful experience for both mentor and protégé.

Mentoring to Greatness

As I grow older, I pay less attention to what men say. I just watch what they do.

—Andrew Carnegie

Adding a mentoring level to the demands and responsibilities of the ensemble conductor may seem weighty, but in a sense, it is unavoidable since mentoring is already taking place at least on the passive level. The conductor that would welcome the positive activity of intentionally mentoring a protégé must be observant, respect the fact that observation is taking place, and be prepared for the "teachable moment" in the life of the protégé.

The proverb states, "When the student is ready, the teacher will arrive." Even though the entire ensemble is watching, observing, and learning, not every single performer in the ensemble is looking for a mentor, so the conductor does not have to behave as if everyone is an intentional protégé. The fact remains, however, some would like to be.

When the protégé arrives, the mentor-protégé relationship will not be about lesson plans, or syllabi, or course outlines, or lectures. However, every encounter and potential lesson drawn from experience will matter to the protégé. Every choice, decision, style preference, and other characteristics and traits will take on new meaning for the protégé.

For the mentor, the experience must always be about the protégé. The mentor invites the protégé along on the journey for the sake of the lessons, the future good of the calling, and for generativity within the vocation. The reward comes in the fuel given by the mentor to the protégé for the lesson, and the lesson well received and applied by the protégé. Benchmarks are those moments when a lesson becomes life for the protégé. Reinforcement takes place when the mentor affirms the work of the protégé and further gives the protégé a chance to teach or apply the lesson observed and learned.

The mentor that accepts the request to work with a protégé, and that is willing to share strategic, technical, cultural, and other important lessons, should make an outline that anticipates the development, change, and eventual ending of the formal aspect of the mentorship. To keep the process objective, the careful mentor will schedule periodic reviews or times of reflection and evaluation for the protégé, with both mentor and protégé working out of the journals they are both keeping. When appropriate, the mentor may involve a third-party participant to help with various aspects of the mentorship and to add an objective, outside voice and perspective.

A good plan for ending the mentorship is to determine the shape of the ending and the process for ending the mentorship from the beginning. As mentor and protégé discuss guidelines and structure at the outset of the process, they can agree on a timeline that includes the point of termination. Collins advises, "Ending a successful mentoring relationship can be harder than walking away from a failing one, but recognizing when it is right to take this step is important."

For the protégé, the termination of the mentorship can take place with the statement, "Thank you for taking the time to work with me. I appreciate all of your time and attention." James Hunt makes the point that serving as a mentor is "an act of citizenship." Protégés participate as good citizens in this process by thanking their mentors for their time, energy, and assistance, and for contributing to their transition into their new level of understanding.

While completely optional, the ending of the mentoring process can be symbolized by the giving of an object to the protégé, or to the mentor, that has acquired meaning throughout the process. In the musical art, such symbolic objects can take the form of a concert ticket stub, a printed program, a baton, a calendar, or any object that may have been part of a lesson or experience during the mentorship that holds symbolic meaning.

The "thank you" that terminates the mentorship remains with the protégé throughout life whenever referring to a mentor. For the mentor, the experience remains a lifetime legacy as the protégé carries on the work, with the mentor wearing the mantle of generativity through an appreciative protégé.

The Continuous Mentor

Mentoring is who you are as much as what you do.
—John Maxwell

Research by Johnson and Ridley demonstrates that individuals interested in the process of generativity and the nurturing and care of protégés actually make excellent mentors. With this in mind, anyone exploring this topic out of personal interest in the process of mentoring is appropriately self-selected, and most likely very suitable for the journey and adequately prepared for the experience. This willing tendency and trait appears to be part of the personality of the individual, and continues throughout his or her career. Further, it appears that this trait cannot be taught or trained. This research strongly suggests that if a person is drawn to mentoring, then most likely he or she has gifts to be one.

This further suggests that the rewards for such individuals must be intrinsic, with the mentor finding motivation within the satisfaction received from helping a protégé move along in his or her career and life. While extrinsic rewards may appear from time to time for the mentor, the ongoing interest in this process is primarily motivated by intrinsic rewards, and this is certainly the case for the conductor-mentor as practiced in the musical arts.

Additional traits of individuals interested in the mentoring process include transparency, emotional stability, and affability. Mentoring for such individuals becomes a way of life and essential parts of their professional skill set. For the person interested in being a mentor, it is difficult to *not* mentor.

For those that do not show an initial interest in the mentoring process, it is important to realize one of the basic premises of this book, which is that mentoring takes place in the musical ensemble setting, regardless of the conductor's intentions. The conductor that retreats from the idea of an intentional mentoring relationship will still benefit from creating the mental dashboard of the intentional mentor.

Outstanding mentors are self-reflective and self-aware. To be a truly effective mentor, it is imperative that you be mindful of your own congruency. Knowing that a protégé respects a mentor that is able to say, "I don't know," can be a helpful corrective for a mentor that is tempted to go beyond his or her level of expertise. It is what the mentor already knows and accomplishes that makes for a significant mentor, not what the mentor thinks he or she needs to know.

The Ensemble as Mentor

I've learned that people will forget what you said, people will forget what you did, but people will never forget how you made them feel.

—Maya Angelou

In the 21st century environment of flat organizational charts and increased emphasis on the collaborative workplace, the ideal mentor may emerge as a coalition of peers, including fellow ensemble members, a personal learning network, other supervisors, workplace subordinates, and colleagues of equal rank, all mentoring each other.

Current thinking toward building a personal learning network is to gather a small group of five to six individuals who take an active interest in a person's professional development. Labeling this group a personal learning network describes both a physical gathering of individuals, as well as the possible virtual gathering of learning resources through blogs, Web sites, RSS feeds (Really Simple Syndication), social and professional networks, Twitter, and the many other digital sources.

The challenge of mentoring through a personal learning network lies clearly in defining what the protégé desires to gain from the mentoring circle. The advice is, limit this list to four or five objectives in order to clearly maintain focus and accountability. For the protégé in this mentoring network, the task is to clearly articulate what you seek to learn, how the schedule will function, and how often you will meet or encounter the individuals or group of individuals.

Clearly, some encounters will be more beneficial than others, and just as clearly, some lessons hold a higher priority than others. The desire to learn and mentor remains the same for a protégé looking to a personal learning network as it is for the protégé looking to an individual mentor. Returning to Gladwell's revelation and insight regarding who and what is interesting, important lessons can come through average situations and sources.

The value of group mentoring is that the activity is reciprocal and democratic. Every protégé contributes to every other protégé. This new model of mentoring is one of reciprocity. This does not mean, however, that the contributions made within the group have to be equal. The amount of time the group devotes to each individual can be determined by how much he or she is receiving, how much he or she is giving, and by the complexity level of lessons.

Thought Experiment

Reflecting on the concept of personal learning network, consider the experience of a group known as "The Inklings."

For nearly two decades between the early 1930s and the late 1940s, a group of literary individuals called "The Inklings" gathered informally in Oxford, England, to learn from each other in their narrative fictional writing, and to encourage each other in the writing of fantasy. The more regular members of this ensemble of writers were faculty members at Oxford University. The group included such notable writers as J. R. R. Tolkien, C. S. Lewis, and Charles Williams. Until late 1949, The Inklings' readings and discussions occurred during Thursday evenings in C. S. Lewis's college rooms at Magdalen College. The Inklings and friends were also known to gather informally on Tuesdays at midday at a local public house, The Eagle and Child.

The principal purpose of meetings was to hold readings and discussions of the members' unfinished works. Among the novels first read among The Inklings were Tolkien's *The Lord of the Rings*, Lewis's *Out of the Silent Planet*, and Williams' *All Hallows' Eve*. Not only did these authors and teachers work at one of the most prestigious learning institutions in the world, they also valued the importance of mentoring in a personal learning network as they advanced their own writing.

The concept of such personal learning networks is obviously not new. But taking the initiative to create such a learning network within the musical ensemble, or outside an ensemble, may be a novel concept. The fact is, within the ensemble are many individuals with shared interests and values and who invest a considerable amount of discretionary time in the same pursuit. It could be a very good place to start.

Life and the Question "Why?" as Mentor

Mentor: Someone whose hindsight can become your foresight.
—author unknown

Leonardo da Vinci kept a notebook and wrote his ideas down, no matter how trivial or inconsequential. He tied his notebook around his waist and it served as his constant companion. In one margin he wrote he was taking a break from work "perche la minestra si fredda" ("because the soup is getting cold"). Sure, it is a great reason to stop, but why write it down? And did he think that anyone would read it? But that was what he did. Seemingly, no idea was trivial to Leonardo.

Leonardo observed everything. His famous notebook pages reveal hundreds of pictograms, sketches, phrases, musical notes, drawings, and other reflections. Not only did he observe, he intentionally observed. He made time in his life to ponder. We know this because he wrote it down. Leonardo's most often used word was "perche?"—"why?" You find this word over and over again in his writings. One entry begins, "Perche li cani…"—"Why does a dog…" It was not enough to observe, but he also questioned "Why?"

Leonardo posed difficult challenges to himself. He gave himself tough tasks such as to describe the tongue of a bird or the experience of thirst. He was not afraid of problems and might even be described as a problem creator—but those problems were for him to ponder and for his own disciplined mentorship of life. The evidence demonstrates that once he identified the problem, through observations, sketches, and experimentation, he sought a solution to it.

I reference the habits of Leonardo because these are the same habits of the mentor and the protégé. The mentor is consumed by "perche"—"why"—and the protégé is asking the same question. When we deal in terms of "why?," we want to know the original motivation, and all of the mechanical questions that follow, like "what?" "where?" "when?" and "how?" Mentors are engaged in every one of these important pursuits, but the question of "why" remains the prime motivator in most purposeful individuals, and unites the mentor with the protégé.

Most of us in the musical arts are life-long protégés to the same degree as Leonardo. While Leonardo is thought of as a visual artist and musician, for income he pursued military contracts. We are tempted to think of Leonardo not only as the iconic "Renaissance Person," but also as something of an ideal human being. However, Leonardo was very real and came from humble and ordinary circumstances. He was raised between two homes. His famous practice of writing backward has been explained as a possible example of dyslexia, or possibly evidence of being self-taught in reading and writing. Leonardo did not complete some of his visionary projects. In fact, he started a lot of things he never finished. But he started them. He pursued them. In the end, he never achieved his life's dream to fly.

Leonardo's vocational title on any given day could have been military contractor, inventor, painter, or musical entertainer. Leonardo was certainly practical, but he was also a dreamer. His lists ran from useful to fantasy. Leonardo was very human. He loved people, work, play, food, and life. He was at the same time protégé and mentor.

How could Leonardo have ever learned the essence of all of those vocations, or the skill set for any one of those vocations, from a single person or a single source? It would have been impossible.

Leonardo traded in doubts and questions. He signed his work, "Leonardo Vinci discepilo della sperentia"—"Leonardo Vinci, Disciple of Experience." Leonardo asked "why?," then sought answers, and then wrote down his observations.

Becoming a disciple of experience is the work of the mentor and the protégé. Sharing in those experiences is the reward for mentoring in the musical arts.

REFERENCES

Bennett, William J. (1993). *The Book of Virtues*. New York: Simon and Schuster.

Berthrong, John H. (1994). *All under Heaven: Transforming Paradigms in Confucian–Christian Dialogue*. Albany: State University of New York Press.

Boy Scout Handbook (1965). New Brunswick: Boy Scouts of America.

Bozeman, Barry, and Mary K. Feeney (2007). *Toward a Useful Theory of Mentoring: A Conceptual Analysis and Critique*. Athens: University of Georgia.

Bramly, Serge (1988). *Leonardo: The Artist and the Man*. New York: Penguin Books.

Chuang, Pi-Hua (2005). *The Conductor and the Ensemble—From a Psychological Aspect*. University of Maryland, DMA Dissertation.

Collins, Elizabeth (2008). *360º Mentoring*. Cambridge: Harvard Business School Publishing Corporation. Article Reprint No UO803B.

Collins, Jim (2001). *Good to Great: Why Some Companies Make the Leap and Others Don't*. New York: HarperCollins.

Colvin, Geoff (2008). *Talent is Overrated*. New York: Penguin Books.

Conway, Colleen M., Michael V. Smith, and Thomas M. Hodgman (2010). *Handbook for the Music Mentor*. Chicago: GIA Publications.

Csíkszentmihályi, Mihály (2008). *Flow: The Psychology of Optimal Experience*. New York: Harper Perennial.

Eby, Lillian T. (1997). Alternative forms of mentoring in changing organizational environments: A conceptual extension of the mentoring literature. *Journal of Vocational Behavior* 51(1).

Eby, Lillian T., and Tammy D. Allen (2002). Further investigation of protégés' negative mentoring experiences: Patterns and outcomes. *Group & Organization Management* 27(4).

Eby, Lillian T., and Marcus Butts, Angie Lockwood, and Shana A. Simon (2004). Protégés' negative mentoring experiences: Construct development and nomological validation. *Personnel Psychology* 57(2).

Edwards, Randy (2000). *Revealing Riches & Building Lives*. St. Louis: MorningStar Music Publishers.

Erikson, Erik H. (1959) *Identity and the Life Cycle*. New York: International Universities Press.

Gladwell, Malcolm (2009). *What the Dog Saw*. New York: Little, Brown and Company.

Greene, Robert (2000). *The 48 Laws of Power*. New York: Penguin Books.

Homer (1961). *The Odyssey*. R. Fitzgerald, trans. New York: Doubleday.

Johnson, W. Brad, and Charles R. Ridley (2004). *The Elements of Mentoring*. New York: Palgrave Macmillan.

Kelehear, Zach (2006). *The Art of Leadership: A Choreography of Human Understanding*. Oxford: Rowman & Littlefield Publishers.

Kram, Kathy E. (1985). *Mentoring at work: Developmental relationships in organizational life*. Glenview: Scott Foresman.

Kram, Kathy and Lynn A. Isabella (1985). Mentoring alternatives: The role of peer relationships in career development. *Academy of Management Journal*. 28(1).

Kushner, Harold S. (2006). *Overcoming Life's Disappointments*. New York: Anchor Books.

Levine, Stuart R., and Michael A. Crom. (1993). *The Leader in You*. New York: Simon & Schuster.

Maxwell, John C. (2008). *Mentoring 101: What Every Leader Needs to Know*. Nashville: Thomas Nelson.

McManus, Stacy E., and Joyce Russell (1997). New directions for mentoring research: An examination of related constructs. *Journal of Vocational Behavior*. 51(1).

Newsweek Magazine. December 28, 2009.

Nicholl, Charles (2004). *The Flights of the Mind: Leonardo Da Vinci*. London: Penguin Books.

Noe, Raymond A. (1988). An investigation of the determinants of successful assigned mentoring relationships. *Personnel Psychology*. 41(3).

Pink, Daniel H. (2009). *Drive*. New York: Riverhead Books.

Pipher, Mary (1996). *The Shelter of Each Other: Rebuilding our Families*. New York: Ballantine Books.

Ragins, Belle R. (1997). Diversified mentoring relationships in organizations: A power perspective. *Academy of Management Review*. 22(2).

Ragins, Belle R., John L. Cotton, and Janice S. Miller. (2000). Marginal mentoring: The effects of type of mentor quality of relationship and program design on work and career attitudes. *Academy of Management Journal*. 43(6).

Scandura, Terri A., and Chester A. Schriesheim. (1994). Leader-member exchange and supervisor career mentoring as complementary constructs in leadership research. *Academy of Management Journal*. 37.

Shea, Gordon F., and Stephen C. Gianotti. (2009). *Mentoring: Make it a mutually rewarding experience*. Axzo Press: www.axzopress.com.

Shore, Zachary (2008). *Blunder: Why Smart People Make Bad Decisions*. New York: Bloomsbury.

Singh, Val, Divindra Bains, and Susan Vinnicombe. (2002). Informal mentoring as an organizational resource. *Long Range Planning*. 35(4).

Stanley, Ralph (2009). *Man of Constant Sorrow*. New York: Gotham Books.

Tepper, Bennett J. (1995). Upward maintenance tactics in supervisory mentoring and nonmentoring relationships. *Academy of Management Journal*. 34(4).

Tolstoy, Leo. (1885). *Where Love Is, God Is*. www.online-literature.com/tolstoy/2892/

Wing, R. L. (1979). *The I Ching Workbook*. New York: Broadway Books.

Young, Angela M. and Pamela L. Perrewe. (2000). What did you expect? An examination of career-related support and social support among mentors and protégés. *Journal of Management*. 26(4).

Zey, Michael G. (1984). *The Mentor Connection*. Homewood, IL: Dow Jones-Irwin.

ABOUT THE AUTHOR

Tim Sharp (BM, MCM, DMA) is Executive Director of the American Choral Directors Association (ACDA), the national professional association for choral conductors, educators, scholars, students, and choral music industry representatives in the United States. He represents choral activity in the United States to the International Federation for Choral Music (IFCM).

Sharp, himself an active choral conductor, researcher, and writer, has varied his career with executive positions in higher education, recording, and publishing. Prior to his leadership of ACDA, Sharp was Dean of Fine Arts at Rhodes College, Memphis, TN, and earlier, Director of Choral Activities at Belmont University, Nashville, TN.

Tim's research and writing focuses pedagogically in conducting and score analysis, and various published essays betray his eclectic interests in regional music history, acoustics, creativity, innovation, and aesthetics. He has conducted university, community, church, and children's choirs, and continues to serve as a choral conductor and clinician in the United States and internationally.

Tim resides in Edmond, OK, with his wife Jane and daughter Emma.